Engendering
Democracy in Chile

american
university
studies

Series IX
History

Vol. 201

PETER LANG
New York • Washington, D.C./Baltimore • Bern
Frankfurt am Main • Berlin • Brussels • Vienna • Oxford

Annie G. Dandavati

Engendering Democracy in Chile

PETER LANG
New York • Washington, D.C./Baltimore • Bern
Frankfurt am Main • Berlin • Brussels • Vienna • Oxford

Library of Congress Cataloging-in-Publication Data

Dandavati, Annie G.
Engendering democracy in Chile / Annie G. Dandavati.
p. cm. — (American university studies. Series IX, History; v. 201)
Includes bibliographical references and index.
1. Feminism—Chile. 2. Women in politics—Chile. 3. Women and
democracy—Chile. 4. Women—Chile—Social conditions.
5. Chile—Politics and government—1973-1988.
6. Chile—Politics and government—1988- I. Title. II. Series.
HQ1236.5.C5D358   305.42'0983—dc22   2004014120
ISBN 0-8204-6143-1
ISSN 0740-0462

Bibliographic information published by **Die Deutsche Bibliothek**.
Die Deutsche Bibliothek lists this publication in the "Deutsche
Nationalbibliografie"; detailed bibliographic data is available
on the Internet at http://dnb.ddb.de/.

The paper in this book meets the guidelines for permanence and durability
of the Committee on Production Guidelines for Book Longevity
of the Council of Library Resources.

© 2005 Peter Lang Publishing, Inc., New York
275 Seventh Avenue, 28th Floor, New York, NY 10001
www.peterlangusa.com

All rights reserved.
Reprint or reproduction, even partially, in all forms such as microfilm,
xerography, microfiche, microcard, and offset strictly prohibited.

Printed in Germany

For
Mahantesh and our sons
Rohan and Armaan—always

Table of Contents

Acknowledgments .... *ix*
List of Abbreviations .... *xi*
Introduction *1*
    The Study of Women's Movements in Latin America   3
    The Chilean Women's Movement   6
    Institutionalization of the Movement   9
    Organization of the Book   12

The Cultural-Ideological Plans of the Military for Women *17*
    The PDC and the Centros de Madres   18
    The Allende Government and Women   22
    Changes with the Coup   24
    Secretaria Nacional de la Mujer (SNM)   30
    CEMA-CHILE   32
    Voluntariado Nacional   33

The Socio-Economic Policies of the Military Government *37*
    "Chicago," the Family and Women   39
    The Raw Materials for the Organizations   46
    The Paraguas (Umbrella) of the Oppressed   48
    The Growth of a Democratic Culture   52

The Women's Movement and Women's Organizations in Chile *59*
    The Feminists   60
    Women and Human Rights   64
    The "Survival" Groups   67
    Buying Together (Comprando Juntos)   69
    The Communal Kitchens (Ollas Comunes)   70
    The Private is Public and Political   71
    Diversity in Organization but Unity in Action   74

The Women's Movement and the Rise of the Democratic Opposition *79*
    Protest, Rejuvenation and Unified Opposition   80
    Political Parties and Social Movements   83
    The Wisdom in Strategizing   85
    Women, Political Parties and "No"   88
    Concertación Nacional de Mujeres por la Democracia (CNMD)   90
    The "Wooing" of Women   92

Courting the Human Rights Lobby and the Pobladora — 95

Women, the State and Civil Society ***99***
Women and a "Gender-Responsive" State — 100
No! a la Impunidad: Women and Human Rights — 105
Survival Groups and the State — 107
Internal Division: Indigenous Women and the Women's Movement — 109
Políticas: Women and Political Parties — 110
Feministas: Women and Change in Civil Society — 114
Feminist Organizations and Consciousness-Raising — 117
Campaigns, Conferences and Celebrations — 121

Conclusion ***127***
The Women's Movement and the Transition to Democracy — 128

Bibliography ***135***

Index ***151***

Acknowledgments

Engendering Democracy in Chile has grown out of close to 14 years of following Chilean politics. It is based in initial fieldwork started during the writing of my dissertation and followed by several trips to Chile in the course of teaching here at Hope College. I thank Chilean activists, academics, female militants of political parties, *pobladora* women and professionals in SERNAM for the information they provided through formal interviews, conversations and written material through the years. I am grateful to the leaders and members of the *ollas comunes,* the human rights groups and the professionals from various NGOs for sharing their experiences with me. I thank all these women (they are too many to enumerate here) for giving me their time, energy and insight.

This book represents the culmination of my interest in Chile that was first generated by Professor John McCamant at the Graduate School of International Studies at the University of Denver. The research support provided by Hope College and the Political Science Department has been invaluable in the completion of this project. Marty Jordan, Eleanor Douglass and Mike Ryckman provided excellent and timely research assistance with library searches, editing and computer support, thus providing the final impetus for getting the manuscript to the publisher. I owe a great deal to my father, who never underestimated the power of women and for that and who I am today, I shall always be grateful to him. Finally, I thank Mahantesh, Armaan and Rohan for being a ready source of unconditional love and support. You guys are the best.

Annie G. Dandavati

Abbreviations

AD	Alianza Democrática
ADM	Agrupación de Mujeres Democráticas
AFDD	Agrupación de Familiares de Detenidos y Desaparecidos
CD	Concertación por la Democracia
CEBs	Comunidades Eclesiais de Base (Christian Base Communities)
CEM	Centro de Estudios de la Mujer
CEMAs	Centros de Madres (Mothers Centers)
CEPAL	Economic Comisión on Latin America
CIDEM	Centros de Información de Derechos de la Mujer
CNI	Central Nacional de Informaciones
CNMD	Concertación de Mujeres por la Democracia
COC	Comando de las Ollas Comunes
COCEMA	Confederación Nacional de Centros de Madres
CODECO	Consejo de Desarrollo Comunal
CODEM	Comité de Defensa de los Derechos de la Mujer
CODEM	Comité de Derechos de la Mujer
COPACHI	Comité por la Paz Chilena
COREDES	Consejo Regionale de Desarrollo
CpS	Christians for Socialism
CT	Consultora Técnica
DINA	Dirección de Inteligencia Nacional
DOMOS	Centro de Formación y Servicios de la Mujer
FOSIS	Fondo de Solidaridad e Inversión Social
FUMPO	Frente Unitario de Mujeres Pobladoras
ILET	Instituto Latinoamericano de Estudios Transnacionales
JAP	Juntas de Abastecimiento y Control de Precios
JUNAEB	Junta Nacional de Auxilio Escolar y Becas
MD	Mujeres Democrática
MDP	Movimiento Democrático Popular
MEMCH	Movimiento pro Emancipación de la Mujer Chilena
MF	Movimiento Feminista
MIEL	Mujeres Integradas por Elecciones Libres
MMS	Movimiento de Mujeres por el Socialismo
MOMUPO	Movimiento de Mujeres Pobladoras

MUDECHI	Mujeres de Chile
NGO	Non-Governmental Organization
NSM	New Social Movement
ODEPLAN	Ministry of Planning and Cooperation
OEP	Organizaciones Económicas Populares
OMIDES	Organización de Mujeres pro Desarme, Integración y Desarrollo Latinoamericano
PAIS	Partido Amplio de Izquierda Socialista
PC	Partido Comunista
PDC	Partido Demócrata Cristiana
PEM	Programa de Empleo Mínimo
PET	Programa de Economía del Trabajo
PNAC	National Program of Nutrition
POJH	Programa de Ocupación para Jefes de Hogar
PPD	Partido por la Democracia
PRN	Partido Renovación Nacional
PRODEMU	Promoción y Desarrollo de la Mujer
PS	Partido Socialista
RIDEM	Red de Información de los Derechos de la Mujer
SERNAM	Servicio Nacional de la Mujer
SERPLAC	Secretarias Regionales de Planificación y Cooperación
SNM	Secretaria Nacional de la Mujer
UCHM	Unión de Mujeres de Chile
UDI	Unión Demócrata Independiente
UMS	Unión de Mujeres Socialistas
UP	Popular Unity

Introduction

The rise of authoritarian governments and the process of democratization in Latin America witnessed the growth of social movements. In Chile, the defeat of the military regime is fairly recent and research on the connections between social movements and the democratic transition is limited. But the dynamics of the social movements that characterized Chilean society are important precisely because they played a crucial role in challenging the military government.[1] This book is an attempt to clarify and highlight the rise, development and institutionalization of the women's movement in a Chile moving slowly and cautiously from authoritarianism to democracy. It also seeks to throw light on the impact of the women's movement on the process of democratization.

In the not so very recent past, protest was not even regarded as a legitimate topic of study because the dominant paradigm of modernization did not take political and social conflict into account. The focus of modernization theory lay on political parties, institutions, political culture and economic growth leading to modernization.[2] When the study of protest and movements of protest did become acceptable in mainstream political literature they were explained by either using classical theories or resource mobilization theories. Cohen (1985) writes that the classical theoretical paradigm (made popular by the Chicago School) has an implicit bias, since it regards collective behavior as an irrational response to change. The classical theorists (Kornhauser, Smelser, Davies, Gurr) do not provide us with plausible explanations for the rise of the women's movement in Chile because they consider social movements a response to stresses within society; they define individual discontent that results in social movements as a psychological rather than a political phenomenon (McAdam, 1982). The psychological ramifications of social movements are important but so are the social and political dimensions of discontent and the collective behavior that results from it.

The resource mobilization theorists, collectively known as the Michigan School (McCarthy and Zald 1973; Tilly 1975; Gamson 1975; Jenkins and Perrow 1977: Oberschall 1979), explain social movements in terms of organization, interests, resources, and opportunities. However, they emphasize elite involvement and consequently underestimate the crucial importance of the mass base in the birth of social movements. In the ease of Chile the role of political elites was quite limited: the women's movement arose in the absence of supportive political parties and other elites as well, since many of those who would have supported them were either detained, killed, disappeared or exiled. The movement was grass-roots in origin and derived its strength from the rank and file. This is not to dispute that individual leaders or elites were not involved, but their role should not be overestimated at the expense of popular initiative. Melucci (1985) claims that resource mobilization theory reduces every collective action to the political level and thus, misses the cultural orientation of the emerging social conflicts. It does not give due consideration to solidarity, collective identity, consciousness and ideology. Resource mobilization helps us in understanding how different elements converge to result in conflict but it does not explain the "why" element.

For the Marxist paradigm, social protest is not a "deviant" occurrence as it is for the mainstream theorists; consequently, it represents a step forward in our understanding of conflict. However, the primacy that it accords to class struggle at the cost of other forms of oppression and social change limits the paradigm from explaining conflict that is not class based. The Marxists allocate an extremely important historical and theoretical role to the working class which is charged with the responsibility of being the agent of social change. So while providing us with the language for understanding social and political conflict, the paradigm's contributions are self-limiting.[3] Marxists emphasize the role of workers as "historical agents" who usher in social and political change, but in reality we see that new social actors, such as women, are the harbingers of change. They introduced new ways of doing politics, and non-violently opposed authoritarian regimes. Besides, Marxism does not focus explicitly on the "Woman Question." It helps explain class conflicts in "economic" terms but as Paramio asserts, the

> problem of women does not have its origin in the economy, or in the class struggle, it is a problem of domination ... this domination has not been invented by capital, nor does it have any relation with the structure of classes in society. (1985, 83)

The Marxist paradigm recognizes and concedes significance only to those organizing along "production lines" and in the "workplace." It does not help explain the rise of women as social actors who are organizing not in the workplace, but around private and community issues: human rights and relations within the family.

Thus, the existing paradigms (Marxist, Classical and Resource Mobilization) provide us with limited tools and language to intelligently comprehend the rise of social movements of women, let alone make predictions about them. This leaves us with the West European literature on social movements that expounds on the nature of social movements in advanced democratic capitalist societies.[4] The European New Social Movement (NSM) literature has limited application to Chile, since it entails an analysis of democratic and capitalistic nations not subjected to authoritarian military regimes and not characterized by high degrees of repression, poverty and turmoil. Few studies examine gender-based protest and defiance specifically or even consider gender as an analytical concept or a focus of contention and resistance. However, the European studies do provide us with the tools and the language to understand and conduct empirical studies of these movements. The literature provides us with a preliminary reflection on the concepts and meaning of these movements and it is this paradigm that the present study on the Chilean women's movement will utilize.

The Study of Women's Movements in Latin America

In the past four or five years some work has been done on Latin American social movements in general and women's movements in particular. Commenting on Navarro's article on the *Madres de la Plaza* in Argentina, Eckstein argues

> that gender may, analytically, be of consequence in two distinct ways: as a social base of mobilization and resistance and as a set of issues around which men as well as women can press for change. Concretely, of course, the two may be interrelated. However, while women often mobilize for men's and household concerns, men infrequently mobilize for issues defined as women's concerns. If anyone struggles for "women s issues," it is generally only women. (1989, 26)

Two ground-breaking studies give us a gendered account of the transitions to democracy in some Latin American countries.[5] Jaquette's (1989) book presents case studies from Argentina, Brazil, Chile, Peru and Uruguay establishing that women's movements arose in Latin America in response to authoritarian governments. These movements, while neither strictly liberation nor revolutionary in nature, arose in transitional societies, societies making a gradual move from repressive authoritarian regimes to democratic governments.

The causes responsible for the rise of the women's movements are best discovered by examining the socio-economic, political and human rights environment of the countries under discussion: authoritarian governments, massive human rights abuses, radical changes in the economic structure and drastic political transformation of the state led to the intensive mobilization of women.

Besides highlighting the causes of the rise of a women's movement in each nation, Jaquette's book also identifies the factors which facilitated this massive mobilization of women. Alvarez's (1990) comprehensive ease study of Brazil specifically identifies four factors leading to women's movements: the Church, the Left, the stereotype notion of women's apolitical actions and the existence of other women's organizations. Chuchryk's pioneering study on Chile illuminates the period of the dictatorship and focuses on the rise of feminism and growth of women's organizations in the Pinochet period[6] Chuchryk notes that the Chilean women's movement not only vigorously protested human rights abuses but also established a network of women's organizations that sought to deal with rising problems of hunger, unemployment and poverty.

However, our knowledge of the relations between social movements and the state and political parties is fairly sketchy. We know very little about the shift in the women's movement with a transition to democracy in Chile. Did the movement maintain its autonomy, or did it get absorbed by political parties? Was the women's movement successful in gaining "space" for itself in national politics, and what has become of the movement at the present time? Is it in a state of decline or have women's issues been institutionalized in the political culture of Chile?

What I hope my study on the rise of the women's movement in Chile will add to this existing literature is the analysis of the growth of a collective identity amongst women which helps explain the rise and growth of the women's movement in Chile and sheds some light on the relation between institutionalized politics and social movements. The study highlights the gendered aspects of the transition to democracy in Chile while focusing on the interaction between the women's movement on the one hand and the political parties and the state on the other.

Prior to 1973, politically significant social movements were scarce in Chile. This is surprising for a country known for its high level of politicization and a variety of organizations. However, the weakness of civil society and the absence of social movements actually resulted from the omnipotent position of political parties in Chilean polities and society. According to Garretón (1989), the political system constituted the "vertebral column" of Chilean society. Political institutions were stronger than social organizations, and even if social movements arose, they were mobilized and sustained by the political parties.[7] Garretón considers the fact that no social movements existed autonomously in Chile before the coming of the military government as a mark of the strength of political parties and their ability to represent society effectively. All political demands were to be channeled, processed and distributed through the political parties. Even the labor movement (the strongest classic example of the "traditional" movements) in Chile worked this way. The political parties not only enjoyed a great deal of power and controlled a large number of resources, but also determined who would gain access to the state. Parties formed the government and regulated opposition movements as they negotiated with the state. Consequently, prior to 1973, the social base and the political parties were tightly and inextricably knit. Social organizations and independent social actors were weak without the omnipotent and omnipresent political parties and the state.

All this changed with the coup of 1973. Political parties were declared illegal and persecuted. In the absence of institutionalized channels of expression and with the policy of repression pursued by the regime, the opposition disintegrated. Eventually, it fell to the lot of the people, to organize, become independent and express themselves through the growth of a number of social movements. The military government launched a program of "national reconstruction," privatizing the economy, opening national borders to free trade, limiting the state's economic responsibilities and "centralizing" the state's political powers. Regional and local governments were reinstated as the new regime developed, but they were controlled, and their powers were limited, based on a pyramidal distribution of authority.

As this destatization progressed, the regime used existing systems to communicate its ideological agenda. According to Brunner (1983), the political culture of authoritarianism sought to discipline society, depoliticize the media, integrate society via the market, and move the Chilean nation in one particular direction. This direction was determined and colored by the military government's national security doctrine and its concepts of maintaining order, reinforcing the patriarchal system and limiting the role of the state in dispensing social services. In the Chilean case, the authoritarian project of the military was pitted against the desire for a return to democracy, which the various social movements (including the women's movement) espoused. The conflicts which were covert in the beginning owing to repression and terror soon expressed themselves openly by demanding the defense of human rights and individual liberty, questioning the authority of the state, and opposing a government that had almost eliminated social services and the safety net for the poor.

The Chilean Women's Movement

The women's movement in Chile was an expression of civil society which urged a peaceful, non-violent return to democracy. Women struggled to become independent agents involved in determining the direction in which their country would move. They not only protested the political, economic and socio-cultural domination of the military regime, but also sought to transform the existing situation and offered an alternative vision of society based on democracy, equity and horizontal social relations. Touraine argues that "women are transforming, or trying to transform, their status (which is inferior) and their culture (which is private) into an oppositional force against an instrumental and productivist culture" (1988, 15).

The importance of the women's movement lies in the fact that it presented the first organized resistance to human rights violations and the rampant repression undertaken by the regime. The women's movement represented the first symbolic opposition to the regime. Women's base organizations focusing on human rights and survival issues were the very cells nurturing the opposition movement that was to attain overwhelming proportions by 1983. For the first time in Chilean history, women participated as independent actors and took control of their destiny. Women as citizens, or *ciudadanas*, became the agents of change: they not only initiated reform, but underwent a series of changes themselves which raised their individual and collective levels of consciousness. Uniting for the immediate goal of feeding their families, they laid the basis of an opposition that would in due course strongly question and alter the relations of power and domination.

According to Kirkwood (1983, 1985, 1986), the post 1973 mobilization of Chilean women constitutes a social movement because its members had a strong sense of who and what they opposed. They share a collective identity; they have a sense of solidarity and unity as far as common goals are concerned; and they engage in collective action for reforming society.[8] The post-1973 women's movement is extremely important because it led to women participating as autonomous actors in command of their actions and in possession of a cultural model that sought to transform not only the socio-cultural project of the military but also the existing social relations.

The social actors seeking to impose their own particular model are historical agents who can determine the course and future of that society. The women's movement in Chile (thanks to its feminist strand) came up with a theoretical critique of the model proposed by the military government. The critique proposed alternate socio-political relations which would be horizontal, democratic and equal rather than vertical, authoritarian and undemocratic.

However, the Chilean women's movement was more than a reaction to the cultural model of domination and authoritarianism envisaged by the regime: it involved a process of creation as well. It created a body of theory that advocated changing the relations of power and domination through grassroots organizations that sought to establish a society where women's oppression would be eliminated. Critiquing the military regime while proposing a new cultural vision separates the post-1973 women's movement from the earlier mobilizations of women witnessed during the period of the struggle for suffrage in 1947 and women's demonstrations during the military coup and the fall of Allende.

Women introduced a new form of doing politics, a new conception of what constitutes political activity and issues. Earlier, issues related to daily life were not regarded as political. Arizpe writes that

> In the hegemonic political philosophies found in Latin America and other regions one finds that the demands relating to the private sphere are almost by definition excluded from general political demands. Women's implicit demand that the personal should become political is, in this sense, revolutionary. Women are insisting that their demands enter the arena of debate and political negotiation. (1990, xvii)

Pinochet declared in one discourse after the other the traditional role of women as mothers, housewives, good spouses and protectors of the homeland. Feminists introduced a vision of society where women would play an equal role with men in all spheres of life without being subjected to discrimination. This strong clash in cultural visions had strong political and social implications that continue under the democratic government as well.

The fact that the women's movement arose in opposition to the military government highlights its non-institutional or extra-institutional character. Women, as non-traditional actors continue to challenge the conventional way of doing politics and play an important role in the reconstruction of democracy. The movement's place outside the realm of traditional politics is further reiterated by the issues that it brings forth as worthy of mobilization and political action: survival, respect of human rights and gender equality. Women not only introduce new issues to the realm of politics, but they also adopt novel methods of manifesting protest and opposition. They broaden the sphere of the "political" by politicizing daily life. Social movements politicize the social and socialize the political at some level as well. Writing about the women's movement, Slater (1991, 38) remarks about the novelty of making politics by crossing the old established divide between private and public spaces. Living differently and changing society are not seen as separate; the social practices of everyday life have been given political meaning.

These new historical agents seek to establish an autonomous identity of their own and to develop patterns of socio-cultural practice that are distinct and new. They demand the right to participate directly in decision-making and they try to empower themselves with self-esteem and dignity as new actors who have an equal say in the social, political and economic arena. "Movements can be seen as sources for the reconstitution of collective identities and the creation of new public spaces" (Cohen 1983, 105). So the important theoretical characteristic of social movements is not just the existence of a group of people, conscious of a collective identity, but the formation of groups and organizations that function in accordance with a different, alternative and often conflicting cultural model of society.

The main crux of Touraine's theoretical work is that bona fide social movements have an alternative vision of society and struggle to play an important historical role in the creation of a new society and steer the movement of society, in a particular direction. The question is not one of old and new values but between conflicting values (Offe 1987, 88). There is a clash between different models of development and radically different conceptions of society. As far as the internal organization of these new movements is concerned, they are a far cry from the organizational structures of traditional movements. Melucci (1980, 219) writes about solidarity, direct participation, and the experience of collective action in the new movements. There is relatively little social distance between members and the leadership, and, in fact, hierarchical relations of authority, if not absent, are weak and diffused.

Typically, in contrast to traditional forms of political organizations, they do not employ the organizational principle of differentiation in either the horizontal (insiders versus outsider) or the vertical (leaders versus rank-and-file members) dimension. On the contrary, they seem to have a strong reliance to synthesis—the fusion of public and private roles, instrumental and expressive behavior, and community organization—and, in particular, a poor and at best transient demarcation between members and formal leaders. (Offe 1987, 71)

This is borne out by the women's movement in Chile where organizations are based on horizontal rather vertical relations of power. The Chilean women's movement is also a multi-class movement in the sense that it consist of women characterized by differing relations to the economy the society and the polity. Women's demands are not really class-specific, as demonstrated by the demand for respecting human rights.

Institutionalization of the Movement

According to most new social movement theorists, social movements do not seek state power; rather they want to maintain autonomy from the state and other institutions (Fuentes and Frank 1989; Offe 1987; Falk 1987; Cohen 1983; Melucci 1980). The existing literature agrees that social movements are anti-politics, but are simultaneously preoccupied with altering, if not radically changing, the established rules of the game. Despite the autonomy, the solidarity and the direct participation that these movements so zealously guard, they also share some goals with other movements that encourage them to enter into alliances and collaborate for certain common ends. The desire to achieve certain goals necessitates co-operation with the state and some sort of institutionalization of the movement. The literature does not tell us much about these characteristics of social movements and there seems to be a widely held belief that the institutionalization of social movements amounts to co-opting the movement, rendering it practically useless in initiating social change. I would argue that it is important for social movements to find new ways of representation within the state and political parties. In the Chilean context of state and party domination of politics, social movements would be ineffective (as far as initiating change is concerned) if they did not adopt strategies for maintaining their autonomy. However, they must at the same time translate their agenda into public policies by pressuring the state and the political parties. Melucci writes that because of the fragmentation of collective action, social movements can't survive in complex societies without some forms of political representation. The existence of channels of representation and of institutional actors capable of translating into policies the message of collective action is the only condition preserving movements from atomization or from marginal violence. Openness and responsiveness of political representation keep clear an appropriate space for collective action and let it exist. But movements don't exhaust themselves in representation; collective action survives beyond institutional mediation; it reappears in different areas of the social system and feeds new conflicts. (1985, 815)

This does not mean that social movements must turn themselves into political parties. It does mean, however, that they must evaluate realistically the political situation and enter into alliances and negotiations, with the political parties and the state in order to transform their goals into legislation and long-term change that has the support of the state. One way to do this would be through the growth of social movement organizations and networks, as well as a growth in the number of committed individuals. Organizationally, a difference between movement, state and political parties should definitely be maintained, but a flow of individuals and leaders linking all of them together can provide for and maintain a unity of goals and action. In this manner, members of a social movement could mobilize whenever the need arose, and maintain constant pressure for change on the state and political parties.

One case study of a Latin American social movement (Alvarez, 1990) sheds some light on the dynamics of the institutionalization of a women's movement. According to Alvarez, the women's movement in Brazil was successful in creating a space for itself within the Brazilian state, and the state began to be considered not as a foe to women and social change but essentially neutral in orientation and response to gendered pressure. This study of the Chilean women's movement will highlight the movement's interaction with larger political issues, political parties and the state. With the restoration of a democratically elected government in Chile in March 1990, did women maintain the "political spaces" they had managed to conquer with the absence of political parties, or was it politics as normal—as if nothing had changed in the past seventeen years? With the defeat of the military regime, did women "return to the kitchen," having accomplished the task they had set out to perform, or did the installation of the democratic government witness the continued participation of women in specific local and national spaces? How was the increased participation of women in the 70s and the 80s different from the earlier overwhelming participation of women during times of crisis, such as the struggle for female suffrage and women's participation in the downfall of the Allende government?

There are four commonly accepted criteria that characterize a women's movement: (a) it focuses attention on problems that are specific to women; (b) it deals with interrelated problems that are a function of women's oppression and subordination; (c) it is highly organized; and (d) It sustains a sustained set of activities, strategies and movements common to more than just one organization or group (Chafetz and Dworkin, 1986). The term "women's movement" is broad enough to include the diverse manifestations of gender consciousness and the increased mobilization and participation seen in authoritarian Chile. During the military dictatorship women's groups organized around human rights, issues of survival and feminist consciousness. With the transition to democracy some of these groups continue their work, while new ones have been added in the state, political parties and in civil society.

The rise of the women's movement in Chile and the particular shape and form that it assumed can be understood if it is seen as a response to the political, cultural and socio-economic reality of a Chile subjected to military rule. It is this reality that we need to examine in order to comprehend that the response of Chilean women to this crisis was not only unique, but has been and continues to be far deeper, and more persistent than the earlier syndrome so characteristic of Latin American politics. Earlier patterns of women's political mobilization followed this course: limited participation during normal political periods, increased participation during national crisis and a return to the four walls of the house with the end of the crisis. Politics as usual meant a return to male domination and control by political parties and an all-powerful state.

The post-1973 Chilean women's movement was undoubtedly a response to the national reality of the past two decades, but it went deeper and farther than earlier, short-term responses. It launched the first concerted attack against authoritarianism within the family and the nation and it led to the development of a critique of existing society based on hierarchical relations and the birth of a vision of an egalitarian society that was democratic.[9] And, perhaps most dramatically, it made the lasting contribution of introducing the concept of women as "actors" and "citizens" with individual rights into the common, everyday language of the people (Touraine, 1988).

Therefore, besides being "reactive," the Chilean women's movement was also "creative," and it is this characteristic that makes the movement even more meaningful during the transition to democracy. Women had "reacted" to the political, social and economic reality in earlier periods of Chilean history as well. In 1973 women organized against Allende in support of the family and security and against the economic shortages that had become a characteristic part of the regime. Women in the post-1973 period mobilized for practically the same reasons. What was different about the post-1973 reaction is that it was not isolated and temporary but went hand in hand with "creation." It was autonomous and spontaneous as well as multi-class (as opposed to the earlier mobilization of women that was more often than not controlled by political parties and various sectors of society). It also paralleled the growth of women's organizations both at the grass-roots and middle levels. It presented opposition to the military government but continues to flourish and work for change during the current reconstruction of democracy.

With the transition to democracy, Chile witnessed the institutionalization of the women's movement in both the government and civil society. Aylwin's administration successfully established The National Women's Service (SERNAM—*Servicio Nacional de la Mujer*). This created a cabinet-level office that worked to make public policy initiatives more gender sensitive, thereby, highlighting the importance of gender in public discourse. Other women's organizations outside of the government further engendered democracy by demanding specific policy changes. The issue of gender was no longer marginalized to the realm of the private but played an important role in the *Concertacion's* agenda for economic, social and political development. The women's movement together with the new democratic government worked to mitigate the harsh legacy of the military regime; in terms of economics, politics and human rights. The policies that emanated under the Aylwin, Frei and Lagos administrations and the interaction between their governments and women's organizations have resulted in not just engendering democracy in Chile but also building a more pluralistic, participatory, democratic society.

Organization of the Book

The study begins with a description of the cultural project of the military regime regarding women. It analyzes the "official" organizations of the state (before and during the military government) and the vehicles used by the military government to control and win female support. This analysis provides the ideological and symbolic background for the rise of the women's movement. The second chapter delves into the structural factors that help explain the rise of the women's movement in Chile in the post-1973 period, including the political, social, economic and cultural context in which it arose. The socio-economic reality of Chilean women helps explain the existence of various strands within the movement (human rights, survival and feminist groups), which prioritized different goals. I then proceed to show how this mobilization and increased participation of women was different from previous transient mobilizations. The third chapter focuses on the development of the women's movement and describes the various strands and organizations within it, thus, highlighting the diversity of the women's movement in Chile. It also describes the internal organizations and goals of the various groups, providing concrete evidence of the success of the women's movement in demonstrating an alternative cultural model to the one propagated by the military. The fourth chapter examines the politics of transition, the re-emergence of political parties and the interaction between the military regime, the opposition and the women's movement. It examines the issues and the dynamics of negotiation and compromise within the movement itself and between the political parties and the movement.

The fifth chapter evaluates the women's movement as it exists today in Chile and its performance in terms of co-operating with a state that has included women's issues in the "social pact." It also analyzes the relationship between the women's movement, the cultural dimension of the women's movement and Chilean civil society. The book concludes with a summary of the rise, growth and subsequent institutionalization of the women's movement while describing the challenges it confronts in the process of democratic consolidation in Chile.

Notes

[1] An issue that often causes a debate in a study of democratic transitions is whether the rise of social movements and increased mobilization hastens the process of transition or acts as an obstacle by alienating the elite and giving rise to a conservative backlash. Details regarding these arguments can he seen in Alfred Stepan, cd., Democratizing Brazil: Problems a! iransitron and Consolidation (New York: Oxford University Press, 1989) and Guillermo A. O'Donnell et at. eds., Transitions lion, Authoritarian Rule: Prospects for Democracy (Baltimore John Hopkins University Press 1986). In the case of Chile. the role of the social movements in hastening the defeat of the Pinochet government can hardly he refuted.

[2] For an analysis of the limitations of modernization arid dependency theory in explaining the rise of social movements, see Susan Eckstein, ed., *Power and Popular Protest. Latin American Social Movements* (California: California University Press, 1989). For a comprehensive analysis of the shortcomings of the dominant paradigm in explaining protest and the rise of social movements, see Carl Boggs, *Social Movements and Political Power: Emerging Forms of Radicalism in the West* (Philadelphia: Temple University Press. 1986).

[3] For a critique of the Marxist paradigm, see in particular Jean L. Cohen, "Rethinking Social Movements," *Berkeley Journal of Sociology* 28 (1983): 97- 113.

[4] The most well-known of these writers are Alain Touraine, Alberto Melucci, Claus Offe and Klaus Eder.

[5] Jane S. Jaquette, ed., *The Women's Movement In Latin America: Feminism and the Transition to Democracy* (Boston: Unwin Hyman, 1989). Jane S. Jaquette, ed., *The Women's Movement in Latin America: Participation and Democracy.* 2nd ed. (Boulder: Westview, 1994). Sonia Alvarez, *Engendering Democracy in Brazil: Women's Movements in Transition Politics* (Princeton, N.J.: Princeton University Press, 1990).

[6] Patricia Chuchryk, "From Dictatorship to Democracy: The Women's Movement in Chile," in *The Women's Movement in Latin America: Participation and Democracy*, ed. Jane S. Jaquette. 2nd ed. (Boulder: Westview, 1994); "Feminist Anti-Authoritarian Politics: the Role of Women's Organizations in the Chilean Transition to Democracy," in *The Women's Movement in Latin America: Feminism and the Transition to Democracy*, ed. Jane S. Jaquette (Boston: Unwin Hyman. 1989); "Subversive Mothers: The Women's Opposition to the Military Regime in Chile," in *Women, the State and Development*, ed. Sue Ellen M. Charlton et al., (Albany: State

University of New York Press, 1989); *Protest Politics and Personal Life: The Emergence of Feminism in a Military Dictatorship, Chile 1973-1983* (Ph.D. diss., York University, 1984)

[7] This is the central thread of theoretical thinking running through Manuel A. Garretón's work, *The Chilean Political Process*, trans. Sharon Kellum (Boston: Unwin Hyman, 1989). See also Manuel A. Garretón, "Para Una Nueva Cultura Politica," *Mensaje* 308 (May 1991): 122-27. Guillermo Campero agrees with this analysis in his article, "Luchas y Movilizaciones Sociales en la Crisis: Se Constituyen Movimientos Sociales en Chile?" in *Los Movimientos Sociales ante la Crisis,* ed. Fernando Calderon (Buenos Aires: CLACSO, 1986).

[8] These three features are considered to be of the utmost importance in and defining and analyzing social movements. Other Latin American authors such as Guillermo Campero agree with this line of analysis and so do feminist intellectuals writing on the women's movement, most notably Chilean Natacha Molina and Peruvian Virginia Vargas.

[9] I am referring here primarily to Julieta Kirkwood's seminal article "El Feminismo Como Negación del Autoritarismo" (Santiago: FLACSO, 1983).

CHAPTER I

The Cultural-Ideological Plans of the Military for Women

This chapter will start by providing a historical overview of the political participation of Chilean women, highlighting how early women's organizations were overtly controlled by political elites and parties. This control and manipulation reached an all time high with the coming of the military government, which added an ideological dimension to the strategic control of government created women's organizations.

The nascent expressions of Chilean women's political involvement appeared in the early twentieth century, when middle class Chilean women, wholly conscious of their subordinate status, assumed that gaining the right to vote would eliminate existing gender inequalities.[1] Consequently, they formed women's organizations that exerted pressure on the government and political parties, and were granted the right to vote in municipal elections with the passage of decree No. 320 in 1931 (Galvez, 1998). The *Movimiento Pro Emancipación de la Mujer Chilena*—MEMCH, an organization focused on winning complete suffrage for women, arose in 1936.

Multiple strategies were used by Chilean women to win suffrage rights including the formation of study circles and women's clubs, increasing participation within political parties, and the formation of independent "women only" political parties. No political party was willing to advocate the vote for women; the Left feared women would vote conservatively owing to their affiliation with the Catholic Church and their resistance to change, while the Right, believed most women radicals had leftist inclinations, and that granting women the right to vote would amount to a victory for the Left. Ultimately, however, under the presidency of Ibañez in 1949, women were considered full citizens in the Chilean constitution. Law No. 9292, passed in 1949, granted women the right to vote in presidential elections. María de la Cruz, a colorful and charismatic female leader of this time, who was also the President of the *Partido Cívico Femenino*, was elected to the Senate, but was later accused of activities that jeopardized national interests.[2] Although her name was eventually cleared and she was declared innocent, she resigned from the Senate. The years that followed these dramatic events have been referred to by Kirkwood (1982) and later Galvez, (1998) as a "Period of Silence" for women in Chilean politics.

Writers speculate about why this period of intense female mobilization and activity was followed by demobilization and almost total lack of autonomous participation. The two most plausible reasons are put forward by Delsing (1987, 33): "moral feminism" and the strength of Marxist discourse. Moral feminism postulates that the supposed spiritual and moral superiority and strength of women should incline them to leave "dirty" politics to men. By exalting the values of home, motherhood and feminine purity, Chilean culture helps limit female activity to the realm of the private and discourages women from participating in politics. Apparently the embarrassment and emotional trauma forced on María de la Cruz drove home the idea that politics was just not meant for women. Because this period also witnessed the rise of the Left in Chilean politics, with its emphasis on class struggle and class politics, Marxists gave women the message that class revolution should have the utmost priority. With the success of this struggle, all other forms of domination would disappear as well - so it made sense to unite and work against class domination while relegating the liberation of women to second place.

The PDC and the Centros de Madres

Nevertheless, with the formation of the Christian Democratic Party (PDC) and the subsequent presidency of Eduardo Frei in 1964, the issue of women moved to the front burner once again. For Frei's highly proclaimed goal of "Revolution in Freedom" to be a success, he needed to create organizations through which the State, which was enlarging and elaborating its role in all spheres of life, could dispense services and representation to the marginalized sectors of society. The *Centros de Madres* (Mothers' Centers), essentially associations of housewives (*dueñas de casa*), flourished in the urban and semi-urban centers throughout the country. These government created community-based groups sought to provide opportunities for women to participate in national life, decision-making and self-administration.

While other local community organizations, such as *Juntas de Vecinos* (Neighborhood Associations), *Centros de Padres* (Fathers' Centers), *Clubes Juveniles* (Youth Clubs) and *Clubes Deportivos* (Sports Clubs) flourished, only the *Centros de Madres* were completely comprised of and dedicated to women. In 1968, the *Centros* acquired a juridical identity and came to be called "CEMA", which depended directly on the Executive Power for funding and who's President was the First Lady of the Nation.

During Frei's presidency the *Centros* imparted courses on civic education through which the party hoped to diffuse its political ideas. Mothers Centers combined a celebration of women's roles as wives and mothers with a sense of responsibility to the cause of land reform. Their domesticity and benevolence were an important part of support for the administration, as their role was to support their husbands in political participation. One pamphlet from the *Centros de Madres* reads: "The Mother's Center teaches us how to use available resources in order to create a happy domestic life...we learn to prepare and apply ourselves in the role that corresponds to us as women...to help with men's unions, cooperatives, etc."(Tinsman, 2001) More importantly, the *Centros* provided an important "space" for meeting and interaction among women which was essentially their very own; they gained opportunities to leave the four walls of their homes and the meetings were an important and sometimes their only source of recreation.

Clearly these organizations, although made up of women, owed their existence and *raison d'etre* to the political party (PDC). They were funded by the State, so they had to meet the goals and aspirations that the State had set out for women viz. channelizing women's support for the Christian Democratic Party. These organizations served the "political" purpose of involving women as voters and at the same time building allegiance to the party and the political (invariably male) elites that had helped institute them. These women's organizations, therefore, played the important role of promoting the idea that "a good wife understood the importance of the Agrarian Reform and supported her husband's struggles" (Tinsman 2001).

The PDC was instrumental in the gender mutualism campaigns that effected all women in Chile, especially *campesina* or country women. The promotion of these ideals centered on women being housewives primarily, and the majority of men and women recall this as a time when women did not work. On the other hand, gender mutualism provided a fresh image of the couple as a team. Rather than women working in the domestic sphere and men being breadwinners in a separate world, the two were working together to further socioeconomic progress. For the first time women were considered responsible for maintenance of the family income. Mother's Centers helped to spread this gender mutualism within the framework that a good woman was necessarily involved in civic life. As these changes progressed, so did cultural views of sexual relationships. The Christian Democrats were instrumental in bringing family planning to Chile, rural clinics were put into place and began to provide care and education. (Tinsman, 2001) Overall, the Christian Democrats and Agrarian Reform had a profound effect on gender relations in Chile.

Unmistakably the PDC had the largest impact on women's mobilization during the 1960s; however, there were a series of secondary events that likewise impacted the women's movement, specifically the anti-Allende and later the anti-Pinochet movements. Those particular events were the Cuban Revolution, Vatican II, and student protests. (Baldez, 2002) The political order was changed forever in the Western Hemisphere when Fidel Castro and his revolutionary army marched into Havana on January 1, 1959. Although roots of the political left had been established long before the Russian Revolution, "for the revolutionary left, this era was one of hope; for the anticommunist right, it was one of fear."(qtd. in Baldez, 2002, 33) Castro's success gave new insight to the political left of Latin America, strengthening the view that a democratic pathway to power was not necessary and a socialized economy and autonomy from democratic superpowers was attainable through revolutionary violence. With newfound momentum of the socialist left in Chile, the political Center and Right collaborated their efforts to prevent a revolution. Although in the end the Cuban Revolution did not set off a domino effect of leftist insurgencies, it did mobilize women into the political arena in great numbers, both in favor of and against the socialist movement. However, the political Center and Right were not alone in their fight against socialist ideals. The U.S. government maintained its commitment to anti-Marxist foreign policy by funding the Center and Right of the Chilean government—$720 million between 1961 and 1970 (Collier and Stater 1996:310).

> "These transfers funded the development of new programs, electoral campaigns, and a score of miscellaneous covert operations. U.S. aid provided a substantial boost to the efforts of reformers and anti-Marxist forces in Chile, efforts that they would direct partly toward building a base support among women."(qtd. in Baldez, 2002, 33)

Responding to the polarized environment in Latin America, the Catholic Church in the early 1960s condemned Marxism. Therefore, the Chilean bishops held an anticommunist position and wrote in several pastoral letters that, "Communism deprives man of his liberty, suppresses all dignity and morality of the human person; it denies to the individual all natural rights... [and] destroys any bond between mother and child" (Smith qtd. in Baldez 2002: 34).

However by the mid 1960s, the Second Vatican Council had fostered a commitment to social change and reform, and had become more tolerant of Marxist ideology. In Chile, Vatican II influenced the PDC to shift its base of support from the wealthy elites to the poor and working-class people and to embrace new ideas about political and economic development (Levine 1980:23).

Several Chileans became members of Catholic Action, a Vatican sponsored organization dedicated to promoting Catholic social doctrine, their focus "included spiritual guidance, discussion of strategies for economic and social reform, and service work in factories, coal mines, and rural and urban working-class areas" (Smith qtd. in Baldez, 2002: 34). Many of the women who were active in the anti-Allende and anti-Pinochet movements had been involved in Catholic Action. From the early 1960s, Catholic Action had created a close relationship with the PDC, and when President Frei took office, he employed hundreds of its members to work in his administration. However, by the late 1960s Catholic Action split into two radicalized interests regarding the implementation of the Vatican II reforms (Baldez, 2002, 35). Despite the official church lessening its opposition to Marxism, several conservative Catholics, women and men, pursued the anti-Marxist avenue and became vehicles in the war against Allende during the early 1970s.

The youth of Chile were not far removed from the dichotomized society in the late 1960s. While the youthful culture of marijuana and Bob Dylan was entering the scene of the US, it too was pervasive in Chile. The new generation was redefining who they were with new dress, music, speech and questioning the cohesiveness of the family and the traditional Catholic Church. Such attitudes led to the mobilization of students in the universities, calling them to define their political ideology. In 1967, several students took over the downtown campus of the University of Chile. "They demanded socially conscious courses, financial support for working-class students, and greater student and faculty input in university affairs."(Martínez qtd. in Baldez, 2002, 44). Traditional concepts of women's role in society were transformed with the 1960s being the first generation of women who were expected to pursue a career, "in addition to (not in lieu of) getting married and raising families". (Baldez, 2002: 44) Thus, women too participated in the mobilization efforts of the Left, Right, and Center. However, there was little awareness of gender differences, and only later would the feminist consciousness mobilize against the revolutionary rhetoric and patriarchal actions of the Left (Baldez, 2002: 44).

The Allende Government and Women

Under Allende and the period of Popular Unity, CEMA was re-instituted as COCEMA or the *Confederación Nacional de Centros de Madres* (National Confederation of Mother's Centers). The Centers continued their former functions, but their goals were augmented by the "socialist" principles of the newly formed government. They now began to function as support centers in the direct distribution of goods and services.

The Centers assisted the *Juntas de Vecinos* (Neighborhood Associations) in decentralized management and the government in health campaigns, building houses and setting up parks and recreation centers. Women participated in and were trained to serve as inspectors in the *Juntas de Abastecimiento y Control de Precios* (Supplies and Price Associations, JAP), charged with the responsibility of maintaining supplies and combating speculation and black marketing of products. They became increasingly involved in the political activity and program of Popular Unity: participating in the discussion and search for solutions of local problems and dealing with day care centers, polyclinics and the like.

In 1972, the government created the *Secretaría Nacional de la Mujer* (National Secretariat for Women) as an independent organization involved with issues related to women, such as health, day-care and education. However, the coup of 1973 robbed the *Secretaria* of the time, resources and opportunities to initiate change.

Despite this increased female participation, the Popular Unity government clearly did not formulate a specific program to assist the emancipation of women. In fact, Allende and his government perceived women as part of the exploited working class and considered them the faithful *compañeras* of the workers, protecting the family and playing the role of mother and wife, not as a social group that needed policies (Cleary 1987, 58). Interestingly the government regarded a woman as "worker, mother and citizen" in that order and, consequently, women participated in these organizations as workers and not as "women." In conclusion, prior to 1973 no women's organizations were independent, autonomous and completely preoccupied with the specific needs of women.

In 1973, the existing women's organizations came under the absolute control of the military government which sought to manipulate women's political participation in support of the regime. However, before analyzing the organizational and ideological dimensions of the control exerted by the military government on women's organizations, we must deal with the much-believed contention that women provided the essential support that resulted in a victory for the military in the 1973 coup. Traditional literature would have us believe that women are politically conservative and that women's support for the 1973 coup seems to confirm and validate this viewpoint. However, some studies have disrupted this myth by analyzing the feminine vote and concluding that more Chilean women had voted for candidates who offered change as part of their electoral agenda than for those who did not.[3] The circumstances and socio-economic reality of the period help explain why women elected more progressive candidates. Women's support or resistance was very much shaped and determined by the political, social and economic context within which a particular action was taking place.

Keeping in mind the sharp and rigid political polarization by class and the "confrontation politics" of the pre-coup period,[4] it should come as no surprise that women's groups were severely divided on the question of support for the Allende government.

> The polarization along class lines was reflected sharply among Chilean women. Those who may have been moderately conservative now rallied around the extreme Right; women of progressive or liberal orientation moved to the general Left. The women who belonged to the aristocracy or to the upper-middle class saw their station in life infringed upon. (qtd. in Chavkin 1985, 199)

Conservative organizations such as *El Poder Femenino, Frente Democrático de Mujeres* and the *Organización Cívico-Familiar* consisted of upper- and middle-class women who opposed the Allende government, viewing it as a threat to the family, the nation, and traditional values, an obvious backlash against the radical policies initiated by the socialist government.[5] Upper- and middle-class women supported the idea of a coup because they wanted to protect the family, a sense of stability in social life, and the availability of food, medicine, clothing and housing, not because they were conservative. Rumors abounded that starvation was going to be rampant in Allende's Chile. These fears were backed up by a severe shortage of food and economic hardships that seemed to be the order of the day. Fear about the implications of socialism for the family and children played an important role as well. Support for the coup can be explained in terms of socio-economic security and the defense of the family that are extremely dear to Chilean women.

It is also important to understand the role of the media in fanning anti-Allende hysteria. The housewife had easy access to all kinds of information (not necessarily accurate) through the radio, TV, and various "women" journals such as *Eva, Paula* and *Vanidades*.

> The media campaign was quite successful in blurring the distinction between upper-class women, who were stockpiling their pantries from the black market, and the empty-handed lower-middle class and the poor. The Rightists' propaganda proclaimed that it was an all women's problem, since it was the housewife who bore the brunt. It was not an issue between classes: rich and poor women suffered alike. (Chavkin 1985, 204)

A great deal has been made of the "March of the Empty Pots and Pans" and the various tactics adopted by women to scorn the military and the soldiers, accusing them of being "chicken" and not having backbones. The women were used by the opposition and their most crucial role was to prove to the military that they had wide civilian support.

Thus, the activities of those upper- and middle-class women who were demonstrating and inciting the military, mostly supplemented those of their male counterparts. After all, the military coup did receive the initial blessing and support of the Right and the Center in Chile. It was not the women who were primarily responsible for the military coup (there were various other extremely significant factors in play), and though after the coup Lucia Pinochet hailed the Chilean women "whose suffering, humiliation and heroism saved the hope of freedom for Chile," (qtd. in Chavkin 1985, 207) her words were more of a ploy for laying the foundations for female support and loyalty to the junta than anything else.

Changes with the Coup

After the coup, the opportunities for autonomous participation on the part of women were further decreased with the establishment of official organizations headed by the military government. All modes of independent representation, organization and opposition were eliminated and the ones that remained, such as the organs of local government, were now essentially controlled by political appointees. This helped the dictatorship to maintain order at some level; however the regime's punitive system of control widely involved human rights abuses and repressive rhetoric in order to silence any opposition. "There was a double play of signification occurring with the violence committed by the State against the mothers, fathers, wives, husbands, and children that the state considered to be dangerous for the order."(Hines, 2001) In reality, the military government was out to discredit politics and political parties for having caused division and violence in Chile and for being ultimately responsible for the problems of the country. It emphasized centralization of authority in the military, and accordingly provided tightly controlled, hierarchical channels of participation. According to Volk,

> this was to be a key element in the institutionalization of Pinochet's authoritarian plan. It creates the appearance of decentralization, where demands placed on the state would be passed down to, and generally ignored by, local authorities, while power is actually centralized at the top via a network of personally beholden mayors, intendants, and governors. (1988)

It is not surprising that this control was extended to all organizations including those of women and youth.

The *Juntas de Vecinos* and the *Centros de Madres*, which so far had served as vehicles of territorial representation and participation (however, limited, dependent and clientelistic), were now completely controlled. Mayors were appointed by the *Junta*, and consequently, were direct agents of the military. Therefore, the military exercised absolute power over the working of the Municipalities and the representative organizations with the aid of the CODECO (Council of Communal Development). Of course, the CODECOs and the organizations that constituted them were all militarily controlled as well.

The powers of the Municipalities were greatly increased in the process of destatization, or trimming down the powers of the state, and the military reinforced traditional women's roles to further erode local self-administration. The Municipalities now administered, financed and managed the dispensation, provision and privatization of health care, housing, educational facilities and all other public services. However, since they were not genuinely representative, the Municipalities did not function efficiently or in accordance with the needs of the people, and they did not provide channels for autonomous citizen participation. This organizational control was further strengthened by a traditional ideology that defined the "right" role for Chilean women. Although the military government did not create this ideology, it reinforced it with rigidity and carried it to its logical culmination.

The national security doctrine, the dominant ideology of the military government, served as the very basis of the political and social project introduced by the authoritarian regime. The doctrine presented an extremely traditional and reactionary vision of women's "correct" place and contributed to reconstructing a new cultural, political and socio-economic fabric in Chile. Chilean society (like all Latin American societies) is a patriarchal society that defines the concept of "masculine" and "feminine" through a rigid division of labor on the basis of sex. Men are regarded as strong, independent and dominant; they are responsible for providing for the family, functioning in the public sphere and thus, participating actively in the political life of the country. Women, on the other hand, are considered weak, dependent, subordinate, and responsible for raising children and fulfilling all household and religious duties. The conventional view was that since women function chiefly in the private sphere, they should be uninterested in politics.

Thus, the roles of the sexes are defined in a manner that maintains the superiority and domination of men over women. Men exhibit traits of machismo and act in accordance with its norms whereas women function in accordance with marianismo (Stevens 1976). These roles are not only defined in terms of the separation of the realm of the private and the public, but are also based on the assumption that a women's domain is the home and the family. Consequently, women should not be interested in anything else, or wish to exchange the power that they enjoy in the household (in accordance with the sexual division of labor) for increased discrimination and vulnerability outside the home.

Latin American society reinforces this cultural model through social control exercised in the transmission of values through the family, the school, and the workplace. In the case of Chile, this model has a strong and powerful ally in the Catholic Church. Religious women tend to model themselves after the Virgin Mary; submission, passiveness, obedience, and abnegation are valued in and of themselves as feminine virtues. These values and virtues are supposed to render the women morally and spiritually superior to men, to a state of "moral feminism." Women's spiritual and moral strength manifests itself in daily life through sacrifice, humility, passiveness and dislike for immoral, public activities (such as politics). This moral superiority is supposed to serve as some kind of compensation for the otherwise inferior position that women are subjected to in society. The upshot of this system is that women maintain their subordination and submissiveness (*marianismo*) with "pride," while the men express their superiority (*machismo*) with equal pride and justification.

The necessity and the desire to model oneself after the Virgin Mary also renders the concept of motherhood as sacred and worthy of veneration. An important goal for many Chilean women is to emulate the Mother of God and spend their entire life in the service of their children, sacrificing themselves constantly for the sake of their family. Thus, in the process of seeking feminine superiority, some women become the agents and perpetrators of their own oppression and subordination. Most women have internalized these messages and accepted the traditional domestic role for themselves, seeing their world in terms of the care and education of children, cleaning, cooking and keeping the house. The extremely rigid division of labor, the watertight definition of the masculine and the feminine and the blatant separation of the public and the private have been both the cause and the effect of the subordination of women in Chilean society.

Presently this level of inconsistency in gender relations is being influenced by a changing attitude. Although the process is slow, one can see a change in the socialization of women and men. One example is a popular miniseries called *Machos* which airs nightly and is a large part of popular culture. This *telenovela* (soap opera) depicts the life of seven brothers, some of whom are very macho and some of whom are not. Interestingly, the most respectful of the brothers is homosexual. In addition, the brothers (and the father) who are unfaithful tend to be caught and repaid for their mistakes. This is one example of changing values in the culture, and perhaps a lessening grip of the traditional machismo and marianismo. However, at the time of the military regime, the social scene was much the same as it had been for centuries.

With the coming of the military regime in 1973, the cultural model of machismo and marianismo was further exacerbated. Pinochet often referred to the nearly mythical role of women in the downfall of Allende, saying that women had a sixth sense for danger and were necessary for protecting the fatherland like they protected their family and children (Boyle, 1993). Since the woman's role centered around the home and children and was essentially feminine and private, whereas men's role was external and public, the military government used women's reproductive capabilities as a means of domination. The maternal role of women was reinforced and said to be venerable. *Ser esposa* and *ser madre* (to be a wife and mother) were presented as the *raison d'etre* for women. This domination came disguised by the military government as an appeal to the capabilities of women; to manipulate the social construction women were given their role, the regime told them that they were "como guardiana natural de los valores sagrados de la Nación" or the natural guardian of the sacred values of the nation (Hines, 2001).

The primary target of this ideological manipulation were housewives, and its three-pronged attack revolved around the woman as mother-spouse-housewife, fulfilling specific designated tasks and roles in society. It was believed that women should live for others, strive to satisfy the needs of their families, make sacrifices in this worldly life without a desire for material compensation and define their roles in terms of being good wives and mothers.

The adherence to role designation was an essential part of the national security doctrine.[6] If one were to defy this division, the government argued, one would pose a real threat to Chilean culture, and would invite the very collapse of the family, society and the nation. The maintenance of a peaceful, homogenous, harmonious society required functioning within the limits of role designation.

> "The manipulation and evocation of the family for calculated political gain is the conscious manipulation of the social truth that the family is at the core of public stability that the certainty of the easy continuity of the external rests on the security of the domestic unit."(Boyle, 1993)

Because the family seemed to have calculated roles given to each member, it was the primary relationship in which to foster authoritarianism. Furthermore, since the national security doctrine is conceived of as the defense of the nation and all that the nation stands for,

> it emerges as a concept destined not only to protect territorial integrity but very especially to defend the national values that shape the soul or tradition, since without them national identity itself would be destroyed. (Garretòn 1989a, 77)

The maintenance of the Chilean state and civilization allowed no disruption of the patriarchal model that constituted the very "soul" of Chile. Women had to perform their "function" and "role" as it was dictated by the sexual division of labor for the security of the State. In fact, this was an important dimension of the cultural model advocated explicitly by the military as the *protectors* of the Fatherland. The government claimed that in the "internal war" launched by the military in 1973, women had protected society, since they had begged the military to intervene in order to halt the cancerous spread of socialism in the country. The government cleverly combined these two roles, mother and protector, to encourage women to educate their children in accordance with the values of the military regime. As protectors of the homeland, women were required to inculcate values of order, discipline, obedience and love for the country in the children they were raising. On December 4, 1986, *La Nación* commemorated National Women's Day with an editorial stating,

> It is precisely the woman who will have to play a decisive role in the productive continuation of the work of progress and liberty that the government of President Pinochet has carried forward, not only because she was in the vanguard of the struggle to defend the liberty of Chile, taking the first step to combat Marxism, but also because during these years she has closed ranks in defending peace, tranquility, order, and the family. (qtd. in Baldez, 2002: 120)

Oddly, the official discourses of the military regime regarded women as a homogenous group on the basis of their role as mothers, which transcended all other characteristics of women such as class, status and education.

Authoritarianism in the family favors authoritarianism in the state and society. The motherly role was further emphasized because the nuclear family was regarded as the basis of society, and as a kind of a microcosm of the whole nation. Just as the father is the head of the household and the mother-spouse-housewife must be obedient to him, so too must all women be loyal and obedient to the President of the nation who is nothing more than the "father" at the macro level. It is thus not only legitimized but also regarded as part and parcel of the "natural" and "immutable" order of things in society, and its origin is the patriarchal family. The patriarchal family in terms of women and children thus was considered the moral center of the nation. The mother was considered the central axis of society, and this evocation of the family as a core or pillar was essential in maintaining certainty for any regime that was to hold power. In this sense, the dictatorship maintained the home as the model for social order. "In the sinking ship that Chile in 1973 has so often been depicted as, women were to be its saviors."(Boyle, 1993)

The prescribed, elevated domestic role of women neatly dovetailed with the military government's program of National Reconstruction, which entailed the elimination of "politics" from society. From the authoritarian regime's point of view, persons engaging in politics and political activity represented all that was bad and ugly. Women, enjoying a superior morality (*marianismo*) and having greater spiritual strength, together with the armed forces, could become the architects and the pillars of the new society being so consciously built. Thus, the government had a vested interest in the role of women as protectors of the fatherland, dutiful wives and mothers, raising children to be adherents of law, order and security as defined by the military.

To back this ideological dimension, the regime created specific organizations to control women's participation and to ensure support and loyalty for the regime. The official women's organizations were dedicated to women, but they were neither autonomous nor democratic. Instead they sought to reinforce a patriarchal order. Since the support of women was essential for the continued maintenance of patriarchy and the relations of domination and authoritarianism, the dichotomies of private-public, apolitical-political and feminine-masculine were fortified and strengthened.

Based on these divisions, the private became essentially apolitical and feminine as well. Women were told that being feminine meant being apolitical or nonpolitical. So women had to participate in politics, but only in a manner defined by the military. Women, being virtuous and self-sacrificing, were to dedicate themselves to the "service" of the nation. Wealthy and upper class women had to "serve," "volunteer," and perform "charity" work while women of the popular sectors had to be organized and controlled, and their participation "directed" by their more fortunate sisters.

The political participation of women was channeled and controlled through various women's organizations which served as mechanisms of control: lower-class women's organizations were controlled by their upper-class sisters whose organizations in turn were responsible directly to the military itself. An established hierarchy, similar to that of the military, controlled all these organizations, which were blatantly used to manifest loyalty and support to the regime. Lechner and Levy (1984) claim that these official organizations were vehicles for the social and political disciplining of women and served the purpose of reinforcing their subordinate, traditional role.

Secretaria Nacional de la Mujer (SNM)

The SNM (National Secretariat of Women) was instituted by the military regime on the 17th of October, 1973, after a conference of the leaders of the existing women's institutions convoked by the military government.

> The central proposition was to channelize what had been the feminine support for the 1973 coup. It was a way of giving ample space to women's actions who with great self-sacrifice and responsibility had participated in the struggle for the liberty of Chile in the period of Marxism. (Memoria 1973–83)

Silva (1986) writes that the SNM was a state-controlled institution which depended on the government and was presided over by the First Lady. It was attached to the Division of Civil Organizations and it was responsible for the diffusion of the government's ideological agenda. Actually a part of the state apparatus, the SNM was not really a women's organization per se. It did not have base organizations of its own, but worked with the Centers for Women and other community organizations.

The objectives of the SNM, as mentioned incessantly in its publications, were to nourish a national consciousness in women, ensure a correct understanding of the dignity and importance of their mission and diffuse patriotic and family values. SNM sought to empower women to participate fully at all levels of society, establish a center of research regarding the cultural and legal situation of women and promote women's support for the government. The organization was made up of leaders, monitors, professionals and communal (territorial) volunteers. They held courses, discussions, and meetings periodically, and their publications included *Memoria, Amiga, Cuaderno del Profesor Rural*, and other pamphlets and booklets.

Lechner and Levy (1984) are of the opinion that the SNM coherently served only one important function, namely political indoctrination, and they refer to the SNM as the "party of the President" whose members identified more with the leader of the government than with the organization. It held seminars on the traditional role of the woman as an integral part of the institution of the family, talks on the new Constitution, courses on "The Declaration of Principles of the Military Government" and cultural programs.

The SNM declared that its objective was to "highlight the importance of the woman and to cooperate in increasing her ability to better discharge the role of mother, spouse, [and] housewife" (M. E. Valenzuela 1987, 68). The SNM emphasized feminine generosity for social and charitable work, feminine sacrifice and abnegation for the benefit of the family, and the proper raising and political education of children. The upper-class women's organizations served as conduits for the ideological-cultural model of the military, to the poorer women's organizations in particular and to society in general.

CEMA-CHILE

Under the dictatorship the *Centros* were first suspended, and later reinstituted as *CEMA-Chile*, "whose principal objective is to emphasize the integral development of women and thereby contribute to the well-being of the family" (Memoria CEMA-CHILE 1981). Unlike the earlier period, the *Centros* were no longer affiliated directly with the government, but were directly controlled by *CEMA-Chile*, which was a private, non-profit organization that officially subscribed to the ideology of the military government. CEMA became the fundamental mechanism through which women were integrated in to modernization without questioning traditional roles and without causing breaks in the prevailing model of gender relations. (Anales de la Universidad de Chile. Sexta Serie, 5, Octubre 1997 p.3)

The main goals of CEMA, as defined in the *Memoria* of 1981, were the integral development of women and the well-being of the family. The age of the *Centros* members ranged from eighteen to seventy years, and they were generally not engaged in remunerative labor; they were usually housewives. Girls who were younger than eighteen years and daughters of the members were integrated into *Cemitas*, a subgroup for children that espoused similar ideas.

The *Centros* were directed by monitors (who were paid) and volunteers. Most of the volunteers were members of the SNM and served as "direct and personal communication between the government and the citizens" (Valdés 1989, 35*).* The *Centros* met once a week, and once a month *Centros* directors met with the communal delegate. The training of members took place through courses that were directed by the Department of Training of *CEMA-Chile*. The relations between the SNM and the centers were hierarchical, and the latter basically did what the former directed them to do.

As far as the indoctrination in the *Centros* is concerned, there were talks on the new constitution, the plebiscite, Christian values, and patriotism, although CEMA declared that it was apolitical in character. The *Centros* reinforced the traditional role of women and the "naturalness" of familial functions, and emphasized that women rule a private world without politics. The *monitoras* and the volunteers reiterated that if women should participate in politics at all it should be through the *Centros* and in support of the government. Women were encouraged to emphasize their reproductive role for the family, the country, and the continued maintenance and existence of the established authoritarian order. Since the *Centros* catered to poor women, the emphasis on economic activities was great; artisan goods were produced and then sold through the shops and boutiques of *CEMA-Chile*. Due to the poverty and the unequal distribution of wealth in the wake of unbridled free enterprise, poor women depended on the rich and on the *Centros* for economic support. CEMA set up assistance organizations such as "Houses for Adolescent Girls," as well as "Houses for Peasant Mothers," and "Houses for Urban Mothers." The *Centros* also worked in collaboration with the Municipalities. CEMA also ran polyclinics that provided medical care, shops for the sale of basic commodities at cheap prices, and housing facilities for members. The lack of health care, educational and housing facilities, as well as the rising costs of living and the tightening of social services, meant that more and more poor women sought to become members of the *Centros* in order to claim the free benefits membership provided. In 1988 *CEMA-Chile* had 9,837 *Centros de Madres* throughout the country with a membership of 202,835 and around 5,300 volunteers (Presidential Speech 1987–1988 qtd. in Valdés et al 1989, 41).

> Membership in CEMA offered great benefits and it is very probable that a large number of the women joined for the advantages offered. But once convoked for economic interests, they demanded a moral-ideological compromise from the members... Many members left the centers but did not return their identity card and so continued to avail of the benefits. (Lechner and Levy 1984, 30)

In order to put an end to this opportunistic attitude, CEMA introduced a six-month probation period before issuing the identification card. A big pretence was made that CEMA was a select group, and women were in it because they wanted to be.

Voluntariado Nacional

The National Volunteer Service was the third official organization of the Pinochet government that sought to transform women into *Defensoras de la Patria* (protectors of the Fatherland). *Las Damas del Voluntariado* consisted of about 52,000 women volunteers of the middle or upper-class who performed social services and volunteered their labor to help the needy in society. These members were volunteer-collaborators who served as the link between the government and the institutions for which they volunteered.

The members were grouped into forty-nine organizations, and in 1975 they created (on the initiative of Lucia Hiriart), the *Fundación Nacional de*

Ayuda a la Commundiad (National Foundation of Community Assistance) whose real objective was to control all voluntary organizations in a manner that would serve the interests and objectives of the regime. The participation of volunteers in these organizations was structured in accordance with the positions occupied by their husbands in the armed forces and society. The top positions were given to wives of generals and colonels, and it went down the scale in decreasing order regardless of the capabilities of the women concerned. The participation of the wives of military officials was an extension of the duties and responsibilities of their husbands. Volunteer work done by the wives was regarded as a contribution of the Armed Forces to the social and economic development of the nation. The volunteers formed different groups named after colors and were referred to as *Damas de Blanco* (women who distributed milk to children), *Damas de Verde* (who worked with malnourished children), *Damas de Rojo* (who assisted the sickly poor) and *Damas de Rosado* (who helped hospitalized children). This voluntary work was necessary for the implementation of dictatorship, as on the one hand it completed an important clientelistic function (which the Armed Forces did not have the capacity to perform), and on the other hand it contributed to diluting the social conflicts generated by the inequalities of the market (Anales del la Universidad de Chile. Sexta Serie, 5, Octubre 1997 p.4).

The emphasis on voluntary work highlights the fact that women's work was essentially free, whereas that of men was more highly regarded. The fact that Pinochet was the commander of the armed forces and his wife was the commander of the army of volunteers expresses the complementary nature of male and female work, and solidifies the division of labor between the sexes (M. E. Valenzuela 1987, 112). The more than fifty one thousand women involved in volunteer work also replaced the role that a diversity of political interest groups may have played in the social sector. For this reason, more political groups could cease to exist without a visible decrease in social involvement. The volunteers helped maintain a link between the military government and the popular sectors, winning support for the regime and making sure that the patriarchal, authoritarian culture stayed in place.

Under the dictatorship, the *Centros, CEMA-Chile* and the SNM disseminated patriotic values and declared the importance of a woman's traditional role as spouse, mother and housewife. But the existence of these organizations does not constitute the basis for a social movement for women. We can conclude that women belonged to CEMA and SNM, but they did not participate in them; they were a part of these organizations, but they were not the organizations. These organizations did not represent them even if they were specially organized for women. Neither the female members of CEMA and SNM nor the organizations themselves were independent, autonomous "social actors," they were merely executing the needs and will of the military regime.

These women's organizations essentially served as a medium for political indoctrination and social control and as a vehicle for the implementation of certain government programs that specifically targeted women. This was the case with all three governments - the Christian Democrats, the Popular Unity, and the Pinochet government. The only difference lay in the degree of manipulation, indoctrination, and control. In this context, the ideological and organizational control exercised by the military government set the scene for an independent and democratic women's movement, which had its basis in the cultural and socio-economic reality of the period under discussion. This movement presented an alternative vision of society and articulated social, economic and cultural relations diametrically opposed to those advocated by the military government.

Notes

[1.] For a historical account of this participation see the work of historians, members of the Taller de Investigación Histórica "Teresa Flores." Edda Gaviola, Lorella Lopresti and Claudia Rojas, *Queremos Votar en las Próximas Elecciones. Historia del Movimiento Femenino Chileno* 1913-1952 (Santiago: Coedición Centro de Análisis y Difusión de la Condición de la Mujer y Otros, 1986). See also Eda Cleary, *El Papel de las Mujeres en la Política de Chile. Acerca del Proceso de Emancipación de Mujeres Chilenas Durante la Dictadura Militar de Pinochet* (Alemania Federal, 1987); Julieta Kirkwood, "Feminismo y Participación Política en Chile" in *La Otra Mitad de Chile*, ed. María Angélica Meza (Santiago: CESOC, 1985); Riet Delsing, *The Chilean Women's Movement. Reflections on Consciousness, Participation and Power* (M.A. Thesis, The Hague, 1987); Patricia Chuchryk, *Protest, Politics and Personal Life: The Emergence of Feminism in a Military Dictatorship, Chile 1974-1983* (Ph.D.diss. York University, 1984).

[2.] For details regarding this see Chuchryk, *Protest, Politics and Personal Life*.

[3.] For a detailed analysis of this see Mariana Aylwin et al., *Percepción del Rol Político de la Mujer: Una Aproximación Histórica* (Santiago: Documentos Instituto Chileno de Estudios Humanísticos, 1986). See also Steven M. Neuse, "Voting in Chile: The Feminine Response," in *Political Participation in Latin America*, ed. John Booth and Mitchell Seligson (New York: Holmes and Meier, 1978).

[4.] For more on this see David F. Cusack, *Revolution and Reaction: The Internal and International Dynamics of Conflict and Confrontation in Chile*. Monograph Series in World Affairs (Denver: University of Denver, 1977). See also Kenneth Medhurst, ed., *Allende's Chile* (New York: St. Martin's, 1972).

[5.] For an analysis of this support and its genuineness see María de los Angeles, "El Poder Feminino: The Mobilization of Women against Socialism in Chile," *Latin American Perspectives* 4 (Fall 1977): 103-13; and Michele Mattelart, "Chile: The Feminine Side of the Coup d'état," in *Sex and Class in Latin America*, ed. June Nash and Helen Safa (New York: Praeger, 1976).

[6.] For more on the national security doctrine and its implications for the Chilean military, state and society, see Manuel A. Garretón, *The Chilean Political Process* (Boston: Unwin Hyman, 1989); José Comblin, *The Church and the National Security State* (Maryknoll: Orbis Books, 1979); and Robert Calvo, "The Church and the Doctrine of National Security," in *Churches and Politics in Latin America*, ed. Daniel H. Levine (Beverly Hills: Sage Publications, 1980).

CHAPTER II

The Socio-Economic Policies of the Military Government

This chapter will highlight the "historical project"[1] which the military government sought to institutionalize with its coming to power in 1973. In assessing the various aspects of its plan to restructure society it will become apparent that the military's policies adversely affected women and thus, prepared the ground for the rise of an autonomous women's movement. I have already discussed the government's dominant ideology introduced through its official women's organizations. In this chapter the focus is on the economic, social and political policies of the military regime which provided the material context for women's resistance and mobilization.

While delineating reasons for protest and resistance, Eckstein notes that

> ...state institutional arrangements may also be a contextual factor, influencing responses to grievances. The democratic versus exclusionary nature of regimes on the one hand, and state material, symbolic, and organizational resources on the other, influence whether and how discontent is articulated. They affect whether people turn to collective or individual, formal or informal, strategies to improve conditions they dislike. (1989, 39)

Studying the organizational, institutional and policy arrangements of the military government helps develop a more comprehensive understanding of the rise of an independent women's movement in Chile. Much more than the frustration-aggression hypothesis, or other similar arguments claiming to explain the rise of women's protest, changes in the state structures and the policies of the military government went a long way in shaping the responses of the women's movement.

Clearly, the repressive regime's agenda was diametrically opposed to that of the government preceding it. From 1973 to 1978, the regime focused on two main issues: the economy and the elimination of all forms of opposition. The military government was going through its reactive phase, and as Garretón (1989a, 120) writes "Prior to 1978, except for the changes produced by the economic model, there was neither innovation nor new rules of the game but only repression, dismantling, and immobility."

With the coming of the military, repression was rampant and uncontrolled. However, in March 1975, with the launching of the Shock Plan and attempts at institutionalization of the regime, the repression became more selective and centralized. This led to the creation of the National Intelligence Directorate, or DINA. Politically, the regime sought to restructure Chilean society. It depoliticized, fragmented and atomized society, prohibiting any kind of political or social organizations, eliminating opposition groups and movements, declaring the political parties illegal and closing all avenues of interaction between the state and society.

This political model was based on the personalization of leadership. Pinochet went from being Head of the Governing Junta to Head of State and then to being President of the Republic, while continuing to hold the position of Commander in Chief of the Army. He successfully eliminated all opposition within the defense forces, and "accentuated the vertical distance between the Commander in Chief and the newly promoted officers, who owe everything to Pinochet" (Garretón 1989a, 122).[2] The important events prior to the economic crisis of 1981 and the growth of the opposition in 1983 revolved around the Declaration of Principles (1974), the Constitutional Acts (1976) and the *Chacarillas* Plan (1977), all of which sought to institutionalize the regime by writing a new constitution. Pinochet's victories in the national plebiscites of 1978 (regarding a continuation of his regime) and 1980 (involving the acceptance of the new Constitution) are indicative of the success of his control, the fear of repression, and the complete breakdown of the polity and civil society.[3] The government removed all political activity from social life and concentrated it in the hands of key political actors who were also the initiators of "modernization" and "development" through the neo-liberal model.[4] The social costs of giving free rein to the market to determine the efficient allocation of resources were extremely high. A series of studies provide sufficient evidence to conclude that the popular sectors were quantitatively and qualitatively impoverished.[5] Not only did underemployment and unemployment rise during this period, but there was also an increase in the marginalization of the poor.

Socially, the regime closed all avenues of participation and eliminated groups and organizations that articulated social identities and popular growth. It sought to replace the culture of self-help, solidarity and community with fear, conformism and consumerism. It controlled the media and completely disarticulated society. The military implemented its own peculiar organizational model, which

> involved reversing the democratization process and replacing state control of opportunities with new patterns of distributing and concentrating them through the market. The effect was to enshrine a conception of society as a market in which stratification and segmentation appear to be a natural order, the principle of organized collective action is systematically rejected as leading to politicization, and the state loses its identity as the focal point for social demands. (Garretón 1989a, 125)

Thus, the military regime radically restructured the economy and reorganized the polity and society. Both were now organized on an authoritarian and hierarchical basis similar to that of the military.[6]

"Chicago," the Family and Women

Due to economic pressures, increasing unemployment and underemployment as well as declining real wages, women were forced to assist their husbands and supplement the household income. There seemed to be an inherent contradiction in what the government advocated for women and what the social and economic conditions of the period, brought about by the neo-liberal economic experiment of the *Chicago Boys*, demanded from them for sheer survival. The SNM sermonized that women should regard their work outside the home as something temporary; they should be engaged in their true profession (motherhood) and should fulfill their familial responsibilities. Much as the Popular Unity had expected women to support their husbands in land reform, the military government expected women to rally behind the new leadership by fully supporting their husbands as the country was supposed to support its own head, Pinochet. This ideal became more impressed on women and therefore, much more difficult to overcome when the time came to change their tactics in order to move towards democracy. This reaction, of course, is exactly what the military government wanted.

However, more often than not, employment outside the home was not temporary. The reasoning behind this is found in the Chicago Boy's plan for flexabilization of labor. This gave companies the power to use very temporary contracts with their workers and thus led to unemployment and financial insecurity among many families. A laborer may only be able to insure work for around three to six months, therefore women would have to pick up jobs to make up for the unsure income (Interview, conducted May 15, 2003 Maria Theresa Alverez, director of female temporal workers campaign SERNAM). Consequently, there was a dramatic (almost 200,000) increase in the number of female heads of households in this period. Women were increasingly incorporated into the work force either as domestic help or in low-paying jobs of the informal sector of the economy while men stayed home due to increasing unemployment and job competition. This presented a grave challenge to the traditional division of labor, as well as to the assigning of gender-specific roles in the family. To the traditional role of being mother and wife was added one of being the provider and, hence, being responsible for the survival of the family. One of the hidden results of the neo-liberal model was the reversal of traditional male-female roles and the imposition of a "double burden" on women. Women were now responsible not only for providing for the children economically, but also for fulfilling household duties. A considerable loss of self-confidence on the part of men stemmed from their perceived inability to provide for their wives and children. This humiliation, coupled with a reluctance to do "women's work" in the home, led to increased alcoholism, abandonment of the home by the husband and domestic violence.[7]

In the midst of heightened marginalization of the poor resulting from the Chicago model of economics, economic crisis fluctuated within all sectors of the population. In 1982, the debt crisis hit a crescendo in the rest of Latin America. Due to this overwhelming level of debt, nearly all of Chile's banks were forced to declare bankruptcy by 1983. Because of this situation, a deep recession began where unemployment hit 30% (Baldez, 2002, 147). In the opinion of many, this was the beginning of the end for the Pinochet regime, the economic model upon which they had staked success was shown to have weakness, and the damage was not saved for only those who the military had been against, but also to its allies.

Women became extremely aware of their predicament and began to question this division of labor, understanding the double standards and inequalities of the patriarchal model upheld by the military. "Given the extent of repression that Pinochet exerted over Chile—no freedom of the press, no Congress, no demonstrations, no meetings, no opposition—women's quiescence seemed guaranteed. In this context, the emergence of a feminist movement was nothing short of amazing."(Baldez, 2002, 121) The military regime may have advocated traditional roles for women; however the flexibilization of labor and the economic hardship of the neoliberal model obliged them to leave those roles in order to provide for their families. This caused an increased awareness of the public sphere for women, and provided the solidarity needed to catalyze change. Bladez writes: "The punitive effects of regime policies—massive unemployments, price increases, the disappearances of family members—destroyed the private sphere. The fact that the military justified its actions in defense of the family exacerbated this situation and precipitated women's collective action (2002, 162)."

Inequities in the distribution of wealth were exacerbated during the military regime.[8] The results of a study conducted by the University of Chile and Office of National Planning (ODEPLAN) show that in 1985, forty percent of the poorest sectors of the population received only thirteen percent of the national income, the forty percent intermediate received 32.5 percent and the twenty percent of the richest received fifty-four percent of the total income (Hardy 1989, 99).

This gave rise to several different levels of protest. Most famously, the banging of empty pots and pans from within the home became a release for a population to protest even though their behavior was restricted by curfews and they had to stay in their homes. Women gained confidence through these arenas, and soon women's organizations protested for democracy within the home in addition to in the country (Baldez, 2002, 150). New organizations sprouted to help cope with the financial hardship.

Various programs such as the *Programa de Empleo Minimo* (PEM) and the *Programa de Ocupacion para Jefes de Hogar* (POJH) were introduced by the government in order to tackle unemployment and the decline in real wages. POJH was created to provide employment for heads of households. The term "heads of households" meant men (since women could not be legally regarded as heads of households), despite the fact that many women with children did not have husbands, or were the primary income providers in the family. The municipalities which were responsible for implementing these programs put women on PEM. Its beneficiaries received half the salaries of POJH's recipients, since PEM was a minimum employment program, and this, according to most writers doing research on the female work force, went a long way toward "feminizing poverty."[9] In fact, thirty-four percent of the labor force was a part of *Programa de Empleo Minimo* (PEM), and eighty percent of these were women. The monthly salary was no more than twenty dollars, which was not much especially considering that one kilo of bread cost eighty cents at that time.[10]

The economic policies of the government hit women and the lower-income family directly, and not surprisingly, grass-roots organizations dealing with hunger and unemployment rose up. Although the entire family participated in these organizations, they were predominantly made up of and led by women. It would be fair to say that

> even when men, women and children all experience the problems caused by badly built small houses, lack of public services such as water, electricity, drainage, pavements, schools, health centers and popular food centers, or the high cost of living which reduces the possibility of survival, it falls fundamentally to women to manage the income, or rather the poverty. (Damián 1990, 35)

One of the important tasks of the Chilean state prior to 1973 was the provision of social services related to health, nutrition, housing and education. Women, as wives and mothers, were the ones who served as the link between the state (the provider) and the family (the consumer of goods and services). Women were the primary receivers of these services even though they were not necessarily directed at them. If they were the primary clients of the social services provided by the state, they were also the first ones to be hit by the subsequent termination of these services under the military government. Since women link the world of production and reproduction, and the private world of the home and the public world of the community, it is understandable that women led the earliest opposition to the military government.

The health system in Chile under the military government exhibited both modernization and exclusion. Even though mortality rates were low, it is important to keep in mind the social, class and gender context of health service.[11] It was characterized by a decrease in government expenditure on health, the decentralization and privatization of health services, and the increasing cost of services at a time when such services were least affordable. Public expenditure on health care per inhabitant dropped by 22 percent between 1970 and 1983. Public health facilities, representing 53.5 percent of all health services, had to be used by 70 percent of the population, while private health facilities representing 46.5 percent of total health services were catering to only 30 percent of the users. While state spending on public health decreased from 58,000 million pesos to 37,000 million pesos from 1981 to 1987, the dues paid by workers increased from four percent to seven percent of their taxable income (Hardy 1989, 109–10).

The special health needs of women were not given any consideration; education and teaching regarding contraception and birth control were discontinued. While in 1964 only 2 percent of the users of the National Service of Health had regulated their fertility, in 1974, the figure had risen to 20 percent (Cabrera et al. 1975). However, all this was to change with the advent of the military government. In 1979 ODEPLAN (Office of National Planning) issued a document explaining that the military government desired an increase in the country's population, that it rejected the use of contraceptives and sterilization, and that it opposed abortion of any type. The military government also began to enforce the laws against abortion. During the early 1980s, about 1,000 women every year were prosecuted and about a fourth of them sentenced to imprisonment. The majority of these women were pregnant after having been raped and were being punished for attempting their own abortions or for undergoing an abortion (Cook and Dickens, 31). Thus, women's bodies, their sexuality and reproductive capacities were controlled by the state to a large extent, as access to contraceptives became extremely limited. At the same time, the state did not undertake any measures to assist in the "reproduction" of society by providing facilities that would cater to the special needs of pregnant women, newborn infants and children. The health system in place mirrored an androcentric conception of medicine and the peculiar needs of the "feminine condition" were generally ignored (Diaz 1988).

Another of the regime's policies affecting women's health was the removal of nutrition and food programs for minors and children of the poorer sectors. The *Programa Nacional de Alimentación Complementaria* (PNAC) provided milk and food to children and a supplementary diet to pregnant mothers, as well as members of the more vulnerable sectors of society. However, due to improper management, the ones who merited such help the most never got it, leaving large sectors of the population badly malnourished and underfed.

Another grave problem was the lack of housing which gave rise to *tomos*, or land seizures, which in turn led to the development of shantytowns, the two biggest ones being *Silva Henríquez* and *Fresno*, where facilities such as paved roads, electricity and water were completely absent. These encampments manifested the daily, "private" and otherwise invisible drama of homelessness and *allegados* (relatives and friends who share a house). The situation of the *allegados* mainly affected young families with small children. It led to the disintegration of privacy and put an enormous amount of pressure on the nuclear family. Under the military regime, housing was decentralized and the government declared that it was not the role of the state to construct homes and to administer mortgages - only if it was proved that the established channels were not living up to their commitment would the state assume these responsibilities (Kusnetzoff 1985).[12]

In 1973 the housing deficit was about 544,000 homes affecting 27.3 percent of the total families in the country. Fifteen years later it had increased dramatically, affecting 39.8 percent of the total families (Hardy 1989, 128). Around forty percent of the families participating in the *ollas comunes* (discussed in the following chapter) and living in the *poblaciones* (shantytowns) were *allegados* (Hardy 1989, 128).

Under the military regime, the process of transference of administrative, management and financial powers to the municipalities with the purpose of decentralizing the government led to the privatization of educational facilities. In education, as in other social services, the inequalities were immense and increased every day. The upshot of the whole system was a marked deterioration in human capital and the growth of juvenile delinquency, drug abuse and unemployment amongst the youth. Though Chilean women were granted equal access to education, the patriarchal orientation of the system did little to change opportunities for women (Rossetti 1988). Education and the socialization received in schools created feminine and masculine identities. Female students fared better than male students on average, but girls were the first to be pulled out of school to take care of younger siblings, assist in domestic tasks, make a living, or contend with marriage or adolescent pregnancies. Even middle-class women bore the brunt of these inequalities, since women were educated only in areas traditionally regarded as "feminine," and in higher education, men still exceeded women. After their educational careers, professional men not only enjoyed better work conditions, but also made more money than women in similar jobs.

The inferior legal status of women provided another reason for the radicalization of middle-class and university-educated women in particular. The Civil Code declared that wives must live with their husbands, be faithful to them and be obedient. As far as matrimonial patrimony was concerned, the husband owned all wealth and property and there was no common patrimony. Nothing belonged to the woman except for the salary she earned. Consequently, the married woman was considered "relatively incapable," as she could only act on the authority of or while representing her husband as ordered by law. According to potestad marital, a husband's rights over the person and property of his wife were complete and absolute (Malic and Serrano 1988). Mothers may not travel abroad with their children without the permission of their husbands or the authorization of a judge. Further, the law favored men in determining whether his children are truly and legitimately his. The husband also enjoyed complete paternal patrimony: he could take away the children from the mother, determine their futures, and had to agree to their marriages if they were minors. These duties could be performed by mothers only if the fathers were dead or unfit to do so.

The Penal Code established punishment for women who committed adultery, but the law referred only to married women, not men. Abortion was illegal, but fairly common. Chilean law does not permit divorce; it grants a nullification whereby the marriage is declared null and void in a Civil court with the testimony of two witnesses. After nullification, only the salary of a woman is her own property, and consequently, many women who are housewives and do not work outside the home cannot get any support or alimony and find themselves in conditions of extreme poverty. Moreover, men are not charged with the responsibility of providing for illegitimate children; women are ultimately responsible for supporting them. This is a common phenomenon amongst popular classes where *conviviencia* (cohabitation), is the pattern rather than marriage.[13] All this leads further to the feminization of poverty.

It is in the Labor Code where one sees the least discrimination against women in the letter of the law (Malic and Serrano 1988). Its implementation, however, is different: women are excluded from certain jobs, paid less than their male counterparts, not trained in similar skills as men, concentrated mainly in the informal sector and not provided with child care in their absence.

On examining the consequences of the military government's policies, it is apparent that the socio-economic conditions were propitious for the rise of a women's movement. There was widespread discontent over the lack of food, shelter, clothing, health care and education. This bears out Eckstein's proposition that "women's economic marginalization is a factor in their mobilization" (1989, 26). However, the mere existence of these conditions is not sufficient to explain the birth of an autonomous and democratic women's movement; the popular sectors have always faced hardships in Chile. What was new and unprecedented was that the social net, which had always existed to prevent these marginalized people from falling through the cracks, was now removed. The crucial factor in explaining the rise of the women's movement is that the military government's policies inadvertently affected women far more than they did men, precisely because they stood in sharp and absolute contrast to the ideological-cultural model proposed by the authoritarian regime. It became increasingly clear to women that the government paid lip-service to one set of ideas and traditions, but implemented policies which exhibited a lack of commitment to these ideas. The patriarchal model propounded so piously by the military began to show cracks and strains.

To this scenario was added the indigenous strength of the grass-roots movement in the form of the Christian Base Communities, the force of the Peoples Church and the theoretical and ideological counter-critique presented by the feminists. With all of the above ingredients mixed in the right proportions, the Chilean women's movement was born.

The Raw Materials for the Organizations

The important question that arises is how did these grassroots women's groups come into being? Who or what provided the main impetus for their growth? In order to answer this question, it is crucial to understand the primacy of community networks which are an important aspect of the daily life and the socio-economic and cultural realities of Chilean women. Many of these networks are difficult to recognize and separate precisely because they are such a regular part and parcel of the *vida cotidiana* (daily life) that women did not even identify them as being special or peculiar - they just took them for granted. Such groups normally consisted of the family, relatives, friends, neighbors, and extended solidarity groups.

> Assistance constitutes a resource that is always available, a social capital which is offered, or one can resort to in times of need. It is a part of the daily routine ... these acts are not isolated but are integrated into a *red* (network) of social relations that does not work on the principle of a favor for a favor, but the feeling that somebody is always there to count on. (Raczynski and Serrano 1986, 212)

These networks might be strong or weak, equal or unequal and often mobile and constantly changing. In some networks physical and territorial proximity was essential, in others it was not. What was necessary is a certain amount of trust, sharing and a spirit of solidarity. Needless to say, one could belong to a series of different networks and be a part of a number of cross-cutting relations. More often than not, these networks did not have organized formal structures and membership, and they merged or disintegrated with the passage of time. Melucci (1984) writes that social movements include not only "formal" organizations, but also a network of "informal relationships" that connect individuals and groups to one another. These networks were indispensable for the growth of the human rights movement and the "survival" organizations, both of which were predominantly made up of women. Networks were born out of necessity. For instance, women in search of their husbands and children would go from one police station to the other, trying to get some information regarding the whereabouts of their loved ones. They soon discovered that they would keep running into others, who like themselves were unsuccessful in tracking down family members. Soon they would decide to conduct their searches together - feeling strengthened and rejuvenated, no longer alone and feeling sorry for themselves because there were others in a similar predicament. They would go to the parish priest or the lay evangelical workers asking them for assistance, and the latter would recommend that they talk to somebody else, and the networks and groups would keep building. The soup kitchens and community stores had their basis in these networks as well. It was common practice for women to borrow some sugar, oil or milk from a neighbor to return at a later date, or to send one's children to eat at a sister's house when one's spouse had lost his job, or if one had vegetables but no cooking gas to borrow some gas from a neighbor, and return the favor by giving her some of the cooked vegetables.[14] As these daily activities became more frequent and organized they formed the basis for the *ollas comunes* (soup kitchens) and *comprando juntos* (community stores) that were to become an inherent part of the life of the popular sectors.

Although the initiative of people themselves was extremely important, certain legacies from the past were visible in these organizations. The *comedores populares* (popular kitchens) were an integral part of the organizing tradition indigenous to the Chilean labor movement and the popular sectors in Chile.[15] Their roots go back to the organizational and leadership skills developed amongst the populace during the period of the Christian Democrats and Popular Unity.

> It is important to highlight the fact (we observed in our field work) that a high proportion of the leaders of the base organizations (almost two thirds of them) had connections with state or private agencies of promotion in the period prior to 1973, or had exercised responsibilities in institutions of social participation such as the *Juntos de Vecinos* or the *Centros de Madres*. Likewise, most of them were party militants. (Campero 1987, 57)[16]

Although these organizations now existed in greater numbers than ever before (in order to meet the needs of the day) and manifested themselves in different forms - enjoying much greater autonomy and prominence than before - their roots went deep and far into Chilean political and social organizational tradition. It is important to take into account this element of continuity provided by the organizational heritage of the popular sectors in order to understand the rise of women's organizations and the women's movement.

The Paraguas (Umbrella) of the Oppressed

The final impetus that these groups needed to "take off" was provided by the Catholic Church and other externally funded non-governmental organizations (NGOs). The Church provided aid for the victims of repression and the popular sectors which were adversely affected by the economic changes so severely and quickly introduced in Chilean society. Leaders from Protestant, Catholic, and Jewish religious organizations became involved soon after the coup in October 1973 by creating a committee for peace. They were able to coordinate employment and petitions for legal aid and worked in many capacities to improve the human rights situation (Baldez, 2002, 129). Cardinal Silva sponsored the *Comité por la Paz Chilena* (Committee for Peace, COPACHI) in order to provide legal aid and humanitarian assistance to the victims of repression and their families. With the assistance of the World Council of Churches, local offices of COPACHI were established in twenty-two of the twenty-five provinces of the country to offer similar services in those regions. After the political repression was institutionalized with the establishment of DINA in 1974 and the suffering of the poor increased with the weight of the economic model and reduced social expenditure, COPACHI expanded its services.

> It provided technical and financial assistance to 126 small self-help enterprises and 10 rural cooperatives. In Santiago it supported a series of social services closely linked with, or operated by the Church's network of base communities - health clinics, soup kitchens for children, cottage industries, youth clubs, and rehabilitation and counseling centers for alcoholics. (Smith 1986, 164)

The connection between Christian Base Communities (CEBs), the Church and resistance to the military government should be clarified. The CEBs were base communities (existing at the base of the Church and of society), consisting of small numbers of the faithful, normally belonging to the same neighborhood (and thus, homogenous to some extent) who were engaging in Bible study and prayer groups. The CEBs also sought to meet other religious, social and economic needs of the community.[17] The Church and some of its followers became concerned that the CEBs were becoming politicized and too involved in social action instead of focusing solely on religion. The liberation theologians[18] and the lay evangelicals defended these changes by saying that it was impossible to read and practice the Bible without getting involved in the hardship and suffering of the poor struggling for justice. They also contended that the tensions between the institutionalized Church, the CEBs and liberation theology were symptomatic of deeper conflicts within the Church. The "preferential option for the poor" was not only forcing the Church to adopt an antimilitary stance in defense of human rights and to alleviate the economic hardships of the poor but, unfortunately, was also costing it in terms of a decreased following among its richer clientele.[19]

During the Frei and Allende years, the CEBs in Chile did not attract significant numbers of followers due to the expanding activities of social and political organizations associated with political parties (Smith 1980). Though few CEBs existed in Allende's Chile, they provided a base to forge a practical synthesis between liberation theology and socialist political and economic thinking. Some priests and evangelists who belonged to the CpS (Christians for Socialism) made explicit efforts to raise the political awareness of participants in the base communities; they also criticized the Church for not supporting Allende strongly and fully (Smith 1982, 1986). It is important to remember that groups of this nature and with these inclinations were limited in number; in fact, CEBs in Chile had a limited following (as compared to Brazil), since people were more engaged in direct political activity and mobilization. Several political and social organizations provided services and it made sense to join them as opposed to those merely catering to "spiritual and religious growth." Consequently, it would be safe to conclude that before 1973, the CEBs in Chile w ere p resent in a n ascent f orm a nd " a c ombination o f societal c ross-pressures and a lack of felt need among the vast majority of the poor made it difficult for the church to create new religiously and socially vital evangelization programs in low-income areas" (Smith 1986, 162).

The c oming of the military government and the political and e conomic impact of its policies changed the situation radically; it led to an increase in the number of CEBs, which began to perform many more functions than the religious one. "With the aid of newly created church organizations at the national and regional levels, [CEBs] became surrogates for other institutions and services no longer operational in secular society, thus attracting many more participants than during the previous regime" (Smith 1986, 163). They served as havens of refuge from repression and as "spaces" for meeting, interacting, discussing politics, engaging in political activity and focusing on social and community issues.

Pinochet soon called for a closing down of COPACHI on the grounds that it was giving refuge to the Left and assisting the enemies of the state to seek exile elsewhere. Cardinal Silva closed the Committee, but utilizing the same staff, created in 1975 the *Vicaría de la Solidaridad* (Vicariate of Solidarity), which was entirely under the auspices of the Catholic Church. The support provided by the Catholic Church and the *Vicaría de la Solidaridad* was indispensable for the growth of human rights organizations. Human rights groups and the Church supported and protected each other in the face of attack by the government.[20]

The Church continued to function as a meeting place as well as an institution supporting self-help projects and organizing activities, such as the *comprando juntos* and *ollas comunes*, designed to feed people and beat the high cost of living. "Church organizations became known as the paraguas - the umbrella" (Baldez, 2003, 135). The solidarity shown by the Catholic Church was decisive in the birth, growth and consolidation of the self-help groups. More often than not, the initial support or donation to get a group off the ground was provided by the Catholic Church or a particular parish priest. Campero (1987) believes that the Church served as a conduit that linked the organizational activity of the sixties and the early seventies with that which developed under authoritarian rule. It provided not only the "space," but the primary source of leadership and a channel through which foreign aid and services flowed into the country. The connections between the popular sectors, informal networks and the church are further borne out by the following statistics. By 1975, it was estimated that there were at least twenty thousand actively committed lay members in base communities throughout the country[21]; by 1978 the number of teenagers participating was over ten thousand. In Santiago, Mass attendance increased after the coup from 20 percent to 42.8 percent in 1979. Many of those participating in religious programs (especially housewives and young children) also took an active part in the nutrition, health, housing and other community projects associated with the base communities. Such social and religious programs of the church begun after 1973 showed the greatest vitality in working-class areas, especially in urban shantytowns; the principal responsibility for these activities lay with the laity (especially women) and nuns (Smith 1986, 168).

The Church was also the first to show how NGOs could function in opposition to the state. In 1976, when the junta purged scholars from the universities, the Church formed the Academy for Christian Humanism, giving scholars the opportunity to conduct an intellectual critique of the regime and provide the outside world with much needed information regarding events in Chile. Joining forces with the Academy for Christian Humanism in 1979, several educated and professional women joined together to form ASUMA, or Association for the Unity of Women, which provided an outlet for them to surpass the level of their mothers. These women had been involved politically and were ready to break women's traditional roles (Baldez, 2002, 135). The feminist movement then arose as a network of middle class professional women who set up the *Círculo de Estudios de la Mujer*, in 1979 and not only conducted research, but also held discussions on the situation of Chilean women under the protection of the Church. Feminists also sought to increase awareness regarding the subordination of women in society and to promote dialogue between women of different ideological inclinations, disciplines of study and spheres of interest.

The *Círculo* was formed under the auspices of the *Academia de Humanismo Cristiano*, but as its feminist critique developed, it found itself increasingly at odds with a patriarchal-hierarchical Church. A formal split with the Church occurred in 1984 with the formation of the *Centro de Estudios de la Mujer* (CEM), which focused on research and intellectual activity and the *Casa de la Mujer La Morada*, which provided a space for discussions and developed activities and workshops that would lead to increased gender consciousness.

Relations among the political party militants, the Church, the State and the people were obviously not static but constantly changing. Although the Church initially provided space for organizational activity and escape from repression, the organizations and their leaders soon began to see Church ties as constraining the groups' expansion in directions which did not meet with the Church's approval. In addition, the people perceived the Church as paternalistic and unwilling to grant the organizations greater freedom to pursue more political goals (Oxhorn 1991). The government, of course, accused the Church of harboring Marxists and encouraging the enemies of the State. The rise of organizations such as "Tradition, Family and Property," as well as *Opus Dei*, drove home the fact that the richer (and, in that sense, the more important) and more conservative clientele of the Church was not pleased with its activities. These tensions were to become more obvious during the period of the transition, which will be dealt with in greater detail in Chapter five of this book.

The Growth of a Democratic Culture

In addition to the above mentioned "raw material" which led to the rise of the women's movement, a cultural-ideological critique of the military regime and the patriarchal order advocated by it served as the glue holding heterogeneous women's groups together. This critique was developed by Chilean women who identified themselves as feminists. Chilean feminists introduced a theoretical understanding of the authoritarianism in the Chilean nation and family, and sought to sensitize women to the machista-patriarchal culture existing all around them. According to Arteaga, "these women not only questioned the political, economic and social order imposed by the dictatorship, but also the values and ideologies forming the basis of relations in society which were essentially androcentric, exclusive, hierarchical and authoritarian" (1988, 572).

It is not surprising that feminism found its strongest proponents amongst university-educated professional women, for authoritarianism and domination in the universities encouraged resistance and opposition. International connections between Chilean intellectuals and Western feminists, combined with the contributions of women returning from exile with their experiences and feminist ideas, generated new ways of understanding the oppression of the military regime in particular and society in general.[22]

A large number of discussions were held and extensive written material was circulated to sensitize women to the existence of hierarchical and unequal relations which were nurtured and propagated through the mechanisms of socialization in the family and the schools, and held in place through institutions of control such as the family, the Church and the State. One of the themes vital for the rise of feminist consciousness was that the military government sought to impose their authority on all aspects of society. Undoubtedly, women were not the only ones subjected to this authoritarianism, but they were subjected to it at the deepest levels, and they were the ones who could best identify and understand it. They could comprehend it because they had been subjected to authority and hierarchical relations all their lives.

Chilean feminists connected the authoritarianism at the national and the familial level, as well as the structural and political level, and presented an impressive critique of power and the discrimination imposed on women at both levels. Through an awareness of the oppression that existed in their *vida cotidiana*, women could comprehend the inequalities and repression existing throughout the nation. Since the micro and the macro levels were intricately connected, the elimination of dictatorship from the nation was regarded as a necessary prerequisite for changing relations of domination in the family and in society.

The writings of Chilean intellectuals and feminists such as Julieta Kirkwood, Soleadad Larrain, Natacha Molina, Adriana Muñoz, María Antoineta Saa and María Elena Valenzuela among others, sensitized women to the immense contradictions existing in the world of the private; a world that was supposed to be their domain in accordance with gender roles; a world they knew and understood well and were relegated to by a system that was unjust and oppressive. As women confronted problems of keeping their families alive, finding employment, housing and other services for themselves and their children, they recognized how they were being subjected to a repressive system that linked their private and collective experiences. They were beginning to understand that the rigid separation between the private and the public was artificial and unreal.

To women goes the credit of connecting the inequalities characterizing social relations in the private realm to the hierarchical authoritarianism that was a hallmark of the public sphere. The women's movement was the expression of this intricate connection and the desire to change it. Women realized that if they wished to eliminate authoritarianism from society the relations within the family had to change as well. The relation between initiating social and collective change through personal change was established: women sought ways to bridge the gulf between the private and the public.

Women became aware of the contradictions in the patriarchal order that Pinochet and his government were seeking to institutionalize. The hierarchal and personalistic system established by Pinochet reminded women of the unequal relations that they were subjected to within the family. The SNM and the traditional ideology advocated by the military served as a constant personal reminder to women that they were not in control of their own destinies, and that whatever specific role was decided for them, they would always be secondary, controlled and manipulated actors.

If women wished to become independent actors participating not only in the national decision making process but also influencing their own immediate environment (the family), they had to challenge the paternalistic, unified, hierarchical order imposed by the military. Women began to protest against stereotypical notions of their roles in society - roles of being mothers and housewives, roles that restricted their activity to the private realm, and roles that could not and did not permit them to take on the battle against a repressive state. Increasingly large numbers of women began to realize that if respect for life and liberty was to be reinstated in Chilean political and social culture, the military government would have to go.

When women became acutely aware of the situation the dictatorship had forced them into, they were able to identify that male partisanship was creating a roadblock to their cause. Therefore, "women may frame their participation …casting (themselves) as political outsiders, mobilizing in opposition to conventional and male-dominated modes of political engagement. In this case, women framed their actions as a response to men's inability to agree upon strategies to resolve (the) pressing political crisis (Baldez 2002, 167)." This demonstrates resourcefulness and a strong resolve on the part of the women.

The uniqueness of the women's movement lies in the fact that it was not only critical of and opposed to the dictatorship (as several other movements during this period were), but that it was able to establish connections between state authoritarianism and patriarchy and the oppression of women in daily life. It was also the only social movement which considered gender a social category, meriting mobilization, and had goals that specifically revolved around women's issues.

Chilean feminists attempted to provide a language, a discussion and a space essential for women to understand their own particular situation and reality. Women were fighting for control over their lives, their destinies and their decisions. The movement did not have just one goal in mind, although the removal of Pinochet from power was considered to be of the utmost priority. Ultimately, it was the growth of gender consciousness and altering social relations to make them more equitable and participatory that led to the rise and growth of the women's movement in Chile. These unique features have been the primary reasons for the continuance of the movement despite the transition to democracy, precisely because the movement did not owe its *raison d'etre* to the elimination of the dictatorship but focused on women's contribution to creating and sustaining a more democratic polity and society.

Notes

[1.] For details regarding the various aspects of the historical project initiated by the military regime in Chile, see Manuel Antonio Garretón, "The Historical Project of the New Military Regimes in Latin America," in *The Chilean Political Process* (Boston: Unwin Hyman, 1989).

[2.] For a detailed analysis of Pinochet's leadership and his relation with the armed forces as well as the political actions he took to eliminate both institutional and personal opposition within the armed forces, see Genaro Arriagada, *Pinochet: The Politics of Power* (Boston: Allen and Unwin, 1988).

[3.] For more on this see Garretón, *The Chilean Political Process*.

[4.] For an analysis of the economy during this period, see various publications of CIEPLAN and PET. Some of the more important ones are: P. Arellano and R. Cortazar, "Del Milagro a la Crisis," in *Estudios CIEPLAN*, No. 8 (Santiago: CIEPLAN, 1982); A. Foxley, "Cinco Lecciones de la Crisis Actual," in *Estudios CIEPLAN*, No. 8 (Santiago: CIEPLAN, 1982); H. Vega, *Crisis Económica, Estabilidad y Deuda Externa. Un Pronóstico Económico para el Análisis Político*. Documento de Trabajo, No. 33 (Santiago: PET, 1984).

[5.] For more on this see Clarisa Hardy, *Organizarse para Vivir. Pobreza Urbana y Organización Popular* (Santiago: PET, 1988); and *Estrategias Organizadas de Subsistencia: Los Sectores Populares Frente a sus Necesidades en Chile*. Documento de Trabajo, No. 41 (Santiago: PET, 1985). See also Hernán Cortés Douglas, "Stabilization Policies in Chile: Inflation, Unemployment, and Depression, 1975-1982," in *The National Economic Policies of Chile*, ed. Gary M. Walton (Connecticut: Jai, 1985).

[6.] For more on the "militarization of society" see A. Varas, *Chile, Democracia, Fuerzas Armadas* (Santiago: FLACSO, 1980); A. Varas and F. Aguero, *Acumulación Financiera, Gobiernos Militares y Seguridad Nacional en América Latina* (Santiago: FLACSO, 1978).

[7.] For more on this see Teresa Valdés, *Venid, Benditas de mi Padre: Las Pobladoras, sus Rutinas y sus Sueños* (Santiago: FLACSO, 1988); María Elena Valenzuela, *La Mujer en el Chile Militar: Todas Ibamos a ser Reinas* (Santiago: Ediciones Chile y América, CESOC-ACHIP, 1987); Dagmar Raczynski and Claudia Serrano, *Vivir la Pobreza. Testimonios de Mujeres*. 2nd ed. (Santiago: CIEPLAN, 1986).

[8.] For an excellent analysis see Rene Cortazar, "Distributive Results in Chile, 1973-1982," in *The National Economic Policies of Chile*, ed. Gary M. Walton (Connecticut: Jai, 1985).

[9.] See M. E. Valenzuela, *La Mujer en el Chile Militar*; and Raczynski and Serrano, *Vivir la Pobreza*. See also Clarisa Hardy, *La Ciudad Escindida* (Santiago: PET, 1989).

[10.] Virginia Nuñez, "La Mujer Presente en el Combate por la Democracia," in *Mujer y Democracia*, especial-mujer (Santiago: ILET, Unidad de Comuncación Alternativa de la Mujer, n.d.).

[11.] For an analysis of the connections between health, mortality rates and gender, see Ximena B. Diaz, "Perfil de Salud de la Mujer en Chile," in *Mundo de la Mujer: Continuidad y Cambio* (Santiago: CEM, 1988).

[12.] For details regarding the housing policy of the military government see Fernando Kusnetzoff, "Urban and Housing Policies under Chile's Military Dictatorship, 1973-1985," *Latin American Perspectives* 14, no. 2 (1985).

[13.] See Laura Soto, "La Mujer, Ciudadana de Segunda Clase?" in *La Otra Mitad de Chile*, ed. María Angélica Meza (Santiago: CESOC, 1985).

[14.] For a detailed description of these informal networks see Raczynski and Serrano, *Vivir la Pobreza*; and "La Cesantia: Impacto sobre la Mujer y Familia Popular," *Estudios CIEPLAN*, No. 14 (Santiago: CIEPLAN, 1984). See also Guillermo Campero, *Entre la Sobrevivencia y la Acción Política: Las Organizaciónes de Pobladores en Santiago* (Santiago: Estudios ILET, 1987).

[15.] For a detailed account of the connection between the old tradition and the new aspects attained by these organizations, see Campero, *Entre la Sobrevivencia y la Acción Política*.

[16.] This conclusion matches not only my own observations but also my interviews with leaders and members of the *ollas* and the *comprando juntos*.

[17.] For more information on the emergence of the CEBs and their importance, see Thomas C. Bruneau, "Basic Christian Communities in Latin America: Their Nature and Significance (especially in Brazil);" Renato Poblete, "From Medellín to Puebla: Notes for Reflection;" Alexander W. Wilde, "Ten Years of Change in the Church: Puebla and the Future;" in *Churches and Politics in Latin America*, ed. Daniel H. Levine (Beverly Hills: Sage, 1980). See also Thomas C. Bruneau, "Brazil: The Catholic Church and Basic Christian Communities," in *Religion and Political Conflict in Latin America*, ed. Daniel H. Levine (Chapel Hill: University of North Carolina Press, 1986). The ideal for the CEBs' development was an important point of agreement among the Bishops both at Medellín in 1968 and at Puebla in 1979.

[18.] For information on liberation theology, its emergence and chief tenets, its reflections on socialism and Christianity, its spread in Central and Latin America and the tensions between the unified hierarchical Church and liberation theologians, see Gustavo Gutierrez, *A Theology of Liberation: History, Politics and Salvation* (Maryknoll: Orbis Books, 1973); and Alain Gheerbrant, ed., *The Rebel Church in Latin America* (New York: Penguin, 1974).

[19.] For complete information regarding the relation between the Church and various governments in Chile, including the military regime, see Brian H. Smith, *The Church and Politics in Chile: Challenges to Modern Catholicism* (Princeton: Princeton University Press, 1982).

[20.] This chronological list basically follows the events laid down in Natacha Molina, *Lo Femenino y lo Democrático en el Chile de Hoy* (Santiago: Vectro Document, 1986). For example, in May 1986, the *Mujeres por la Vida* demonstrated to show their solidarity to the *Vicaría* which was coming under attack by the military regime.

[21.] The figures are from Brian H. Smith, "Chile: Deepening the Allegiance of Working Class Sectors to the Church in the 1970s," in *Religion and Political Conflict in Latin America*, ed. Daniel H. Levine (Chapel Hill: University of North Carolina Press, 1986). However, Smith writes further that "the estimated 20,000 actively committed laity in CEBs in 1975 constituted a very small percentage of the baptized. Even if this twenty thousand became one hundred thousand by 1980 (a very generous extrapolation), they constituted only 1 percent of the approximately 9 million Catholics in the country" (1986, 169).

[22.] For more on this see Sonia E. Alvarez, "Women's Movements and Gender Politics in the Brazilian Transition," in *The Women's Movement in Latin America: Feminism and the Transition to Democracy*, ed. Jane S. Jaquette (Boston: Unwin Hyman, 1989); and *Engendering Democracy in Brazil: Women's Movements in Transition Politics* (New Jersey: Princeton University Press, 1990).

CHAPTER III

The Women's Movement and Women's Organizations in Chile

In the early period of its growth, the women's movement in Chile was characterized by networks of individual women, who under the auspices of the Catholic Church protested the outrageous human rights violations committed by the military regime. This human rights strand was reinforced by grass-roots base organizations, engaged in helping people survive and building an alternative popular economy of solidarity. Later, the women's movement was characterized by the growth of formal organizations aimed at providing not only a theoretical critique of the existing situation, but also engaging in negotiations with political parties and the state. The movement's growth, however, was not at the cost of losing the complex network of politicized individuals. This linear development resulted from the military government's policies, to which the women's movement was an autonomous, grass-roots response.

Since women from varying socio-economic and political tendencies identified with the movement, it was necessarily heterogeneous. The classes, status, intellectual and institutional affiliations of the movement's members were varied, as were their demands and the causes for their mobilization and resistance. It is important to keep this diversity of interests and goals in mind while dealing with the various segments of the women's movement in Chile.[1] A list of women's groups that existed during the 1973–1990 period is hard to formulate since many of these did not have formal structures or offices and were extremely fluid and flexible.[2] At present, most of these groups have merged with others or have simply disappeared, while others have developed formal structures or are undergoing a process of institutionalization.

Scholars agree that

> the women's movement was in fact a collection of diverse groups with different patterns of organization and different goals. Women's human rights groups were organized by women who were mothers or grandmothers of the disappeared; feminist groups formed to combine consciousness-raising with political and social action; and neighborhood-based organizations of poor women banded together to ensure the survival of their families under increasingly harsh economic circumstances. (Jaquette 1989, 185)

The distinctions between these organizations were not always clear-cut and a great degree of interaction and overlapping occurred. More often than not, the same women were members of more than one group and so categorizing them in this fashion does not suggest that the groups were mutually exclusive.

The Feminists

Analysis of the writings of authors such as Kirkwood, Molina, Valdés and M. E. Valenzuela is essential for an understanding of Chilean feminism. According to Kirkwood, the *problema femenino* (the Woman Problem) has always been understood in terms of the family. A woman's rights have never been advocated as her own rights, rights that are specific and special to her; on the contrary, women have been regarded as the champions and protectors of the family and the fatherland, never as individuals themselves. Consequently, women have always been relegated to the private domain, always spoken of in relation to the well-being of the family, the care and upbringing of children and the maintenance of order in the family and in the nation.

Feminists believed that it was necessary to develop a body of theory and a strategy of *hacer política* (political action) which, according to Kirkwood, must be rooted in women's own social and cultural experiences and needs. Kirkwood argued that women should seek to negate the existence of two separate and exclusive areas of human activity: the public and the private, the former associated with masculinity and the latter limited to the domestic. Women should seek to fight terms such as "unproductive" or "nonworker" as they are applied to them; they must attack the ways "women's problems" are isolated, and confront beliefs that women's demands are temporary and that women are "dependent" and occupy "secondary" or auxiliary positions as "objects" in society. This was important, because within the context of the neoliberal economy, women were compelled to work and thus unable to stick to traditional women's work. Furthermore, they were not respected nor considered qualified to do the menial jobs they were able to obtain, and the conditions of the workplace were deplorable. Thus women needed to be able to consider their traditional roles important in order to see themselves as viable breadwinners (Klubock, 2001, 495).

Chuchryk gives a detailed account of the evolution of the feminist groups which emerged as a result of the political mobilization against the government during the Days of Protest in 1983. On the first day of the protests (May 11,

1983), two women and their children distributed pamphlets saying "Democracy in the Country and in the Home," a slogan that was to become the watchword of the women's movement. By the third day of the protests, eighty to one hundred women initiated an organized feminist opposition to the dictatorship. On August 11, 1983, which also coincided with the fourth day of protest, about sixty women sat on the steps of the National Library of Santiago under a banner that read "Democracy Now! The Feminist Movement of Chile," the first demonstration of a group of feminists that put feminism on the map in Chile (Chuchryk 1985, 26). The most active groups of middle-class women in this period were *Movimiento Feministas* (The Feminist Movement), *Mujeres Universitarias de la Universidad Catolica* (University Women of the Catholic University) and *Mujeres por el Socialismo* (Women for Socialism).

The revival of the *Coordinador de Organizaciones Femeninas* MEMCH '83 (*Movimiento Pro Emancipación de la Mujer*, 1983), which had struggled for the women's vote in 1935–53, was another important landmark in the women's movement in Chile. MEMCH '83 served as an umbrella organization, bringing together various women's groups that opposed the government. Some of these groups were CODEM (Committee for the Defense of Human Rights of Women), MUDECHI (Women of Chile) and AD (Organization of Democratic Women).

Perhaps the most important women's group which arose during this time is the *Mujeres por la Vida*, a group of women of different political and ideological backgrounds that decided to get together in order to protest *por la vida* (for life).

> We are a group of women: a small, weak group, whose principal task is to bring together all the women groups from the political parties and the social organizations to work collectively. (qtd. in Molina 1986, 28)

Its principal objective was mobilizing and maintaining unity amongst women's groups without letting party politics or any other divisive force come in the way. The group did not transform itself into an organization with formal structures, but continued to exist as an informal network. In 1984 the *Organización de Mujeres Pro Desarme, Integración Y Desarrollo Latinoamericano* (OMIDES, Organization of Women for Disarmament, Integration and Development), and the *Centro de Formación y Servicios de la Mujer* (DOMOS) were created. The result of the growth of all these groups was that women got out from the four walls of the home in order to create for themselves a "political space" that had always been occupied by men and the political parties in Chile.

Although feminism was regarded as being wholly middle-class in orientation and in membership, in Chile an increasing number of feminists arose from amongst the popular sectors, making Chilean feminism a multiclass phenomenon. But the feminism practiced by popular class women has been given a name, *feminismo popular* that is indicative of its special socio-economic reality. This distinction results from a combination of class and gender consciousness. Women from the popular sectors are of the opinion that they are doubly oppressed owing to their gender and their lower class status, an exploitation which becomes "triple" for women of a different race or an indigenous group (for example, the Mapuche women in Chile).

Even though class problems in the Chilean women's movement did not appear overt because of the movement's unity in the face of an authoritarian military government, there were tensions under the surface. The needs, demands and priorities of women from the popular sectors were different from those of their middle-class sisters. Some middle class women thought that "class" should be subordinated to "gender," on the basis of which women could be unified as a distinct social group. Women of the popular classes, however, felt that they could not prioritize gender and class. The inability to deal with this conceptual problem and the radical attitudes of some feminists led to the growth of biases amongst popular women who shuddered at the word feminist and regarded it as derogatory. They had their own prejudices which led to the stereotyping of all feminists as "men haters" or "not wanting children or a family."

The most important groups representing popular feminism were Movimiento de Mujeres Pobladoras (MOMUPO), El Frente de Liberación Femenina (FLF), Frente Unitario de Mujeres Pobladoras (FUMPO), Coodinadora Femenina Sindical and other groups such as Las Domitilas and Las Siemprevivas. Perhaps the most important one was El Taller de la Mujer Pobladora. This was an organization of shantytown women who shared problems rooted in the severity of their economic condition. The need to oppose the regime as well as to find means of physical survival and personal growth led to the emergence of El Taller de la Mujer Pobladora. The talleres (workshops) were integrated into eleven Coordinaciones Sectoriales covering different communas (municipalities) of the southern zone.

The membership of those *talleres*, which was completely female, regarded the organizations as providing "space" that is their very own and that offers them an opportunity to interact and share common experiences and problems and have time for themselves without worrying about the family. They learned to value themselves, speak their minds, make decisions independently, experience leadership and assume responsibility. Other organizations, such as the *Domitillas*, also held *talleres* based on women and family, women and society, and women and sexuality. They fought against the dictatorship for an alternative society where women would be respected in the home and in the nation and would be valued for themselves and their contributions to society.

Women joined these *talleres* for different reasons, but soon their desire to comprehend the roots of gender subordination became important.

> The need became apparent to come together as women to talk about women's issues in "women's-only" gatherings, to gain a deeper understanding of the issues they faced... Some of these activities emerged as a natural outgrowth of women's involvement in survival organizations in the community ... others were conceived of as feminist consciousness-raising efforts from the outset. (Moya-Raggio and Zuñiga 1989, 26)

Another way to categorize feminists is on the basis of the "specific activities" on which they focused. Some were engaged in gathering information regarding the situation of women in Chile. They worked in NGOs (nongovernmental organizations) dedicated to this cause, such as *Centro de Éstudios de la Mujer* (CEM). Others worked in foreign-funded organizations, such as *La Morada*, targeting consciousness-raising amongst the populace at large through activist work, and still others considered themselves as having *doble militancia*, viz. feminist members of political parties who chose to work for "women's issues" through the avenue of politics.

The tension between the *feministas autónomas* (autonomous feminists) and the *feministas militantes*, or *políticas* (political-party affiliated feminists) has been one of the chief characteristics of the women's movement from its inception. The *feministas* and the *políticas* had an interesting relationship of both antagonism and of cooperation. The early feminists were normally associated with the political parties of the Left, but their disillusionment caused them to advocate a movement that was autonomous of any kind of political tendency. Consequently, the feminists believed that it was imperative to create their own space specific to women, where it is possible to reflect and develop a critique of women's oppression.

Feminists (*feministas autonomas*) advocated autonomy in the formulation of an agenda that addresses gender issues. They were not opposed to forming coalitions for the introduction of reform and the establishment of a democratic society. But they wanted autonomy to shape and interpret the "women's problem" separately, and viewed the struggle for equality between the sexes as more important than any other. They saw the women's movement as an independent social movement focusing on cultural change within society, rather than on politics. According to the autonomous feminists, if they did not continue to maintain their own autonomous identity, then other organized institutions such as political parties would declare that women's liberation could only come with the liberation of the whole society. Political parties tended to bypass women's issues by declaring that the struggle of women is marginal to other struggles, or that there were more pressing issues that needed to be dealt with before the "Women Question" could be considered.

The militant feminists (*feministas políticas*), on the other hand, considered political parties instrumental in meeting women's demands. They believed that an autonomous feminist movement already existed and increased participation through political parties would improve the effectiveness of women's demands. They declared that autonomy does not signify divorce from politics, that if women's organizations were to remain peripheral to politics, it would truncate and hinder the growth of the women's movement and that women should instead utilize all avenues (including political parties) to achieve their goals. The militant feminists considered their struggle against patriarchy as not being contradictory to the class struggle because the oppression of women is far deeper and more profound than class exploitation and, therefore, they considered themselves a part of the revolutionary process through the practice of feminist militancy.

Women and Human Rights

Since the repression was extremely brutal in the early years of the dictatorship, the goals of the women's movement, as manifested through several of its groups, were largely symbolic in expressing opposition. They were not aimed at obtaining specific demands related either to the group in question or to gender in general, though this was to come later. These early human rights groups aimed at organizing opposition to the regime and creating a public space where this could be manifested. Since most avenues of expression were closed, the Catholic Church played an important role in supporting these groups and serving as a safe haven. The mobilization of women around the issue of human rights politicized what had traditionally constituted the realm of the private. The military would have liked to see women's concerns about family members remain within the family and not get publicized. It was extremely novel that housewives, who prior to this had never been "overtly political," were taking a strong stand on "political" issues. Jaquette writes that

> the unprecedented activism of these women was provoked by an extraordinary cause - the invasion of the private sphere of the family by government which, despite their public commitment of preserving traditional family values, used state terror to maintain political control. (1989, 186).

In 1978, the Chilean Commission on Human Rights (*Comisión Chilena de Derechos Humanos*) was created, as were several *Comités de base de Derechos Humanos* (about one hundred such Base Committees of Human Rights existed in Santiago, with a membership of about two thousand persons). Organizations such as the *Agrupación de Familiares de Detenidos y Desaparecidos* (Organization of Families of the Detained and Disappeared), *Agrupación de Familiares de Presos Políticos* (Organization of Families of Political Prisoners), *Agrupación de Ejecutados en Falsos Enfrentamientos* (Organization of Executions in False Confrontations), and *Agrupación Pro-Retorno de Exiliados* (Organization for the Return of the Exiled) were courageous expressions of reaction to flagrant human rights abuses. Human rights groups, such as *Mujeres Democraticas* (MD), *Comité de Derechos de la Mujer* (CODEM), *Mujeres de Chile* (MUDECHI) and, by far the most interesting of all, *Mujeres por la Vida*, were completely made up of women. The social composition of these groups was multi-class and heterogeneous, as they consisted of victims of the repression, families and friends of victims, political leaders and party militants with diverse ideological beliefs, intellectuals, professionals, housewives and people expressing solidarity.

The human rights groups were predominantly made up of women because men would have to go to work, and women were normally housewives who had more flexible schedules and could go out searching for the disappeared and protesting in the streets. Since men had been more involved in politics, they were primarily the ones who were killed, arrested, tortured or exiled.[3] Chilean culture holds the concept of motherhood with great respect; and some of the rules of the game could be bent for a woman if she was a mother and fitted the traditional feminine role. According to Fisher (1993), it was precisely because they evoked the powerful image of motherhood and the family that women posed problems for dictatorships claiming to defend those same values.

The women working through the human rights groups adopted and introduced new political actions and strategies. They responded to repression and violence with pacifist measures. They used simple methods of protest which defied masculine logic. They chained themselves to the walls of the Congress and CEPAL (Economic Commission on Latin America), trying to arouse the conscience of the world. They wore pictures of their loved ones who had disappeared and carried cardboard silhouettes of the victims of the repression. Chanting various slogans and demanding the whereabouts of their families by asking *"donde están?"* these groups created a large mobilized base against the military regime. They used "simple but acutely effective acts of defiance such as keeping children home from school and permeating the evening air with the din of cooking spoons banging against pots and pans" (Dinges 1983, 15). The *Cueca Sola* was created in 1978 and sung on the 8th of March of the same year in Caupolican. The song testifies to the absence of the male partner for the performance of the national dance. It became the symbol of the group *Conjunto* which was born on March 8, 1978 as well. This period witnessed the growth of the "New Song" movement in Chile, led by singers, dancers and artists opposed to the repression.[4]

Women's politics were "new," since the political actors were housewives who were not supposed to be politically active. According to Lechner (1984), women were introducing and adopting *nuevas formas de hacer política* (new forms of doing politics) because they did not represent a single class. They were asking for something extremely basic - respect for human life regardless of social standing and ideological belief. This was a new experience for Chile where the dominant political actors had been males invested in ideological and polarized class politics. The concept of human rights was a novel idea and to this day it is playing an important role in Chilean politics. It amounted to the introduction of a new ideological dimension in the national discourse.

Women's involvement also entailed a new way of thinking about women's roles. It had never been considered possible that women would step out of the private domain to resist activities conducted in the public realm. But as Moya-Raggio and Zuñiga write these women, in their long years of activities, have radically departed from their traditional roles as wives and mothers, even though these roles enabled them to enter the public, political space ... they have made gains in personal growth, they have gained in confidence and awareness, and they have transcended the private space of their homes to find a niche for themselves ... they came together in defense of life, to reclaim the right of their family members to exist regardless of their political ideas. In the process they created an organization of considerable political and moral influence... Motherhood ceased to be a role enclosed within the privacy of the home; it became a role of broader dimensions, of public visibility. (1989, 19)

Women activists proved incorrect the myths that women are uninterested in politics, incapable of unified action, politically ineffective, passive and resigned to accepting the status quo with very little desire to change things. Ironically, since Chilean society held such strong ideas about women, this actually made women's political presence more effective. Arteaga (1988, 571) points out that human rights organizations were basically a response to the tensions that existed between the State and society at large. Women sought to appeal to the power of the State through the mediation and intervention of organizations such as the Catholic Church. Their opposition amounted to a direct confrontation between the state and its citizens.

The "Survival" Groups

Campero (1987) writes that the *sobrevivencia*, or "survival," groups were not only a defensive mechanism induced by the economic crisis, but also represented a "chain of resistance" and "democratic reserves" which civil society is capable of producing in the face of an authoritarian experience. The strategy selected to combat poverty and hunger was a communal, feminine one: women came together, organized, bought products collectively and cooked together, thus conquering hunger, but at the same time bridging the gap between the private and the public. The upshot of this attempt was the growth of autonomous, mutually supportive grass-roots organizations. Chilean women not only reacted to the hardships they faced, but also created organizations that encouraged popular participation and led to the growth of a parallel popular economy.

The most interesting and widespread reaction to the unemployment crisis was the growth of workshops normally consisting of about three to fifteen workers whose working relations were fairly egalitarian. According to Razeto, "the *talleres laborales* (workshops) are small economic entities whose central activity is the production and commercialization of goods and services" (1990,

54). Most of these workshops owed their existence to the solidarity and material support provided by the Catholic Church and foreign NGOs; however, with the passage of time, some of them were able to function independently.

The workshops utilized fairly simple technology and had very little capital. Some provided continuous and stable employment to a fixed number of workers, and others could only ensure sporadic and partial employment. The outstanding feature of the workshops was that tasks were rotated, and the line of authority was almost non-existent. There was normally a *directiva* (directorate) which determined the tasks that needed to be performed and was responsible not only for dividing the work but also for sharing the resources and profits.

The workshop members were usually housewives and youths, so these workshops provided women who had never previously worked with valuable experience in self-management, increased participation and self-development. The practice of internal democracy within the workshops provided experience in alternative non-hierarchical patterns of social relations. Women were able to interact with one another, comprehend the commonality of their problems and increase gender awareness.

Although these workshops were established with the immediate aim of meeting economic needs, their implications were extremely profound since they had a "whirlpool" effect that crept into the realm of "strategic gender interests." Inadvertently, the workshops provided a structured environment where women could discuss not only their own personal experiences, problems and concerns, but also their perceptions about society at large. The workshops began to serve as "consciousness-raising" groups despite the fact that this was not a task they had originally envisaged for themselves. Women began to see how social and political structures and the process of socialization had assigned them particular gender roles; such a realization had serious social and political consequences.

Amongst the workshops boasting a predominantly female membership, detailed research has been done on the *Talleres de Arpilleras* (Workshops of Sackcloth) where *arpilleristas* (sackcloth workers) used pieces of cloth and thread to make patchwork scenes depicting daily life, poverty, human rights abuses and resistance in Pinochet's Chile. Workshops such as these were not just a place of work but also a place of meeting, interaction and discussion. They sought to eliminate the social and economic exclusion to which women of the popular sectors were subjected, while furnishing them with a means of livelihood.

The foundations formed by these initiatives gave rise to a new understanding of how women could become empowered. They made it clear that it was not only political empowerment or equality in the home that gave women self worth; it was a more complex idea of capability and community. When women were provided with the opportunity to gain skills and form bonds of friendship, they laid the groundwork for a more positive self-image. This idea perseveres today into the women's schools created by PRODEMU, the program for development of women in Chile. These schools give women a venue for development in practical skills, healthy cooking, physical fitness, and self esteem. All of these aspects come together and a women's movement would be incomplete without them.

Buying Together (Comprando Juntos)

Chilean women are culturally and socially responsible for making purchases of food and other necessities in order to meet the needs of the family. With rising prices and unemployment, women had to develop ingenious methods to stretch their *pesos* as far as possible. The result was the *comprando juntos* (Buying Together) groups, "which are based on the criteria of common or collective saving by buying in large quantities so as to obtain the lowest possible prices" (Razeto et al 1990, 63).

The *comprando juntos* did not exhibit as much uniformity as the soup kitchens, since the nature of their functioning depended on the economic level of their membership. Some of the *comprando juntos* conducted fund-raisers in order to gather their initial capital while others created their starting capital by collecting fixed quotas from each participating family. The *comprando juntos* in La Victoria consisted of forty-five groups who were provided their initial capital by CARITAS and consequently the groups' buying power did not fluctuate with the purchasing powers of its members. In other shantytowns, many *comprando juntos* did not enjoy this luxury, and their purchasing power was limited by that of the members of the organization. Some of the *comprando juntos* offered a great variety of products, around forty to fifty, while others provided just the bare minimum. Some with a higher level of economic development were able to accumulate a substantial amount in capital and profits, while others barely survived. Even the manner of distribution of purchased goods differed; in La Victoria, the *comprando juntos* was housed in a room that belonged to the Church. It opened only on Saturday when members could go and buy the products they needed. In other *poblaciones*, where the *comprando juntos* was located in the house of a member, there was no fixed time or schedule for purchase.

Apolonia Ramirez (1986) describes the organizational and popular dimension of the comprando juntos: the members elected a Directorate, which was responsible for buying, maintaining supplies, and keeping accounts. A president coordinated the various functions of the organization. As far as membership was concerned, a majority of group members were recipients of PEM and POJH and, therefore, were mostly women. Members were not remunerated for services rendered, such as bargain hunting, buying the products, transporting the purchased products and working in the store. The organization was of a neighborhood character and worked best amongst people who lived in the same location. Once a *comprando juntos* became successful, it could multiply its functions and increase the amount of its sales and purchases. The advantages of belonging to a *comprando juntos* were many: economical purchasing of essentials, increased savings, membership in an organization, experience in participation and the building of leadership skills.

The Communal Kitchens (Ollas Comunes)

The growth of communal kitchens during the military regime emphasized the inability of the poor to feed themselves, and it manifested the incapacity of the government's social system. The communal kitchens functioned on the concept of collective consumption of food. Food was prepared centrally, and then distributed to all the member and needy families in the *población*. The Church not only provided necessary materials through various agencies affiliated with it, but also made cooking space available. Though the families did not eat in this place, they did get together and cook, not only making collective use of the food provided, but also socializing the private problem of hunger and in the process providing families with food, an act which is culturally considered the responsibility of the head of the household.

The *ollas comunes* managed to impart a certain sense of dignity to the family, as family members ate together in their own home. To some extent, this made an "abnormal" situation more "normal" and acceptable.[5] The *ollas* cooked food from Monday through Friday, and they provided breakfast which normally consisted of milk with rice or oats for children and the aged. The other two meals were for all. All the *ollas* needed were a place to cook, a cooking stove, wood, gas or electricity, raw materials and pots and pans plus fixed family contributions of services such as cooking, distributing the cooked food, washing utensils and maintaining supplies. In the weekly meetings of the *ollas*, all members made plans regarding the cooking and distribution of food, discussed availability and management of resources, solved administrative problems, and developed ties of friendship and solidarity.

Communal Kitchens were important because they socialized the issue of hunger and brought to the forefront the inability of the state to address problems within the community. They also proved to the people that they could come together to provide for one another. The headquarters of the *ollas* were located in Santiago with an estimated membership of 226 organizations consisting of thirty thousand participants. Each *olla* had approximately twenty families with a total of about 120 persons and coordinated its activities with others in its sector. In Santiago itself there were twenty-eight coordinators or sectoral groups. Since 1990, the National Command of Soup Kitchens has been located at Valparaiso (Proyecto Rocap 1991, 7).

The Private is Public and Political

Scholars who have researched popular women's organizations in Chile contend that, while not being the result of a feminist discourse, the *ollas* provided feminist experiences inadvertently, precisely because they represented ruptures in the patriarchal model. According to Hardy, the *ollas* were predominantly female in composition; women made up ninety-three percent of the total membership and eighty-two percent of the total leadership (1989, 187). Women began appearing in leadership roles in their communities, overcoming not only the power exclusion to which women had been relegated, but also questioning the patriarchal order, which was the source of that exclusion. Women came to see the intersection between the authority they were subjected to within the family and the repression that the military and Pinochet exercised over them and the entire nation. The patriarchal order, both within the family and the nation, was being subjected to strains and tensions.

The various grass-roots organizations made "public" the daily life of the poor which the military government considered an essentially private matter. On the face of it, these organizations seemed purely economic in nature, serving the limited purpose of solving the unemployment, housing or hunger problems in the shantytowns. But on close examination, the more subtle political, social and educative dimensions of these supposedly *sobrevivencia* groups become evident. These organizations were the site for a new way of doing politics (*nueva forma para hacer política*). Considering the socio-political and cultural model that the military regime sought to institutionalize, the "protest" or "oppositional" dimensions of these groups which made up the *Economía de Solidaridad* (Economy of Solidarity), were vital. The size of the groups and the absence of any other type of broad, representative organizations of the popular sectors gave them a definite political weight. According to Razeto, "these organizations have a strong aspect of social denunciation and they extend their activities to consciousness-raising about the real situation in which people live in the shantytowns" (1990, 63). Popular organizations served as a school for women's politicization, engendering opinions and ideas that were autonomous of masculine power. They also made public the matters that women faced in personal development, freeing women to become a political force.

> The grass-roots organizations were a place to exercise democracy and self-government for women: rotating responsibility, making collective decisions, direct control of the larger group over the leadership, etc. The ollas were a great experiment: a new form of social organization teaching women to resolve the basic problem of reproduction (feeding), providing alternatives to private and individual solutions and opening a space that is new and particular to the personal and social development of women. (CESIP 1985, 6)

Middle-class women could escape the drudgery and responsibility of housework by hiring lower-class women as servants, and thus, enter the public world. Popular class women did not have this option. However, popular organizations such as the *ollas comunes*, allowed them to reorganize domestic work through the public and collective production of food. In this novel manner, women were able to enter the public world while still fulfilling their responsibilities in the private realm. They were able to make visible the work which they performed on a daily basis but for which they were never given credit. Thus, domestic work was socially valued a great deal more through the activity of these organizations. Using the space allocated to them in accordance with the gendered division of labor, women attained greater recognition for domestic, maintenance and reproductive work. Although popular organizations primarily pertained to subsistence and their chief objective was to cater to the needs of the family, they politicized and publicized hitherto private activities which women routinely performed.

A question of obvious importance revolves around a realistic evaluation of the autonomy of these organizations. Some of the women members of the grass-roots organizations were political party militants, others were not. Some had a long history of participating in social and political organizations under previous governments whereas others were involved for the first time. Many were members of Christian Base Communities. Some members had a highly developed sense of gender consciousness and their subordination and oppression as women, while others declared that feminists were "men-haters." Many of the women were married, while others were single women heads of households; however, the economic situation of all was uniformly precarious.

Generally, the organizations were not financed or directed by political parties and maintained an independent set of goals.

> A good number of these organizations have developed a peculiar sense of autonomy in the context of manipulation by the political parties, the masculine communal leadership and in some case also feminist groups (Vargas 1988a, 15).

These base organizations were the very cells that would nurture the opposition movement that was to attain outstanding proportions by 1983. For the first time in Chilean history, women participated as independent political actors, taking their destiny in their own hands. Women as citizens, or *ciudadanas*, became the agents of change through the series of base groups from which they worked. Through the simple action of coming together to feed and care for their families, they laid the basis of an opposition that would in due course question and change the relations of power and domination in society.

A large number of women participated in anti-dictatorial demonstrations as this period also witnessed the rise of a *poblodora* movement. The grass-roots organizations united and coordinated their efforts with other purely political organizations in the shantytowns, giving an impetus to the *pobladora* movement which was notable for its participation in the National Protests of 1983–1984. Soon the members of these organizations came to realize that democracy was an essential framework for any changes in the social, economic and political conditions of the nation, and a prerequisite not only for increasing social and political participation but also for ending the marginality to which they had been relegated.

We can conclude by reiterating the obvious: that poor Chilean women's lives were full of uncertainty and involved a veritable struggle for survival.[6] The demands and interests of these women were conditioned by their material reality. Furthermore, the survival and maintenance of the family, domestic abuse, violence and sexual issues were all interrelated in a very intricate and subtle manner. Popular organizations were the result of collective solutions and were, in fact, expressions of gender consciousness. They fulfilled specific social needs and had strong political repercussions.

Diversity in Organization but Unity in Action

Despite the differences among the various groups, the women's movement has been characterized by cooperation and collaboration in common activities against the military regime. In December, 1983, the feminists presented the *Demandas Feministas a la Democracia* (Demands for Democracy) which declared that true democracy in Chile could not be possible unless it considered the problems of Chilean women who constitute fifty percent of the population. They declared that discrimination against women was manifested in all walks of public and private life: politics, the law, the work place, the family, the educational system and the state. They also opposed violence against women and advocated the slogan of *Democracia en el País y en la Casa* (Democracy in the Nation and in the Home).

On December 29, 1983, MEMCH'83, *Mujeres por la Vida* and the *Grupo de las 16* (Group of 16) organized a massive demonstration in the Caupolican theater with the theme *Mujeres Hoy y No Mañana, Por la Vida* (Women for Life, Today, and not Tomorrow). The protest was attended by about twelve thousand women. The most important dates on the feminist calendar, March 8 and November 25, were commemorated with enthusiasm and vigor by women from popular organizations, political parties and independent feminists groups. The celebration of these events provided an occasion to mobilize women in collectively denouncing the regime.

Throughout the month of March, 1983, women continued to send letters to accredited ambassadors in Chile informing them about the situation in the country. In April 1984, MEMCH '83 issued a declaration, *MEMCH '83 a la Conciencia de las Mujeres y Hombres de Chile* (MEMCH'83 the Conscience of the Women and Men of Chile). On May 8, 1984, women organized a march in solidarity on International Workers Day. In August 1984, *Mujeres por la Vida* (Women for Life) demonstrated with white handkerchiefs on their heads singing *Gracias a la Vida* (Thank you for life). This was in preparation for the *Jornada Por la Vida* (Day for Life) where once again women participated extensively. Women of all ideological and political inclinations participated in these demonstrations for the defense of life and human rights. The slogan was: *Por la Vida y Algo Mas* (For Life and Something More).

According to Molina,

> 1984 was a year of consolidation (and polarization) for the forces of the political opposition. The existence of the *Alianza Democratico* (AD) and the *Movimiento Democratico Popular* (MDP) imposed a distinct dynamic in the women's organizations. Two different political options began to crystallize with the result that MEMCH was closed to some groups and open to others. (1986, 26)

In September 1984, some organizations such as the MF, MOMUPO and *Comisión de Derechos de la Mujer* (DH) amongst others withdrew from MEMCH'83 on the grounds that the organization was not functioning in accordance with the principles declared in 1983. It had aligned itself too closely with the MDP and women belonging to parties of the Center which constituted the AD were of the opinion that MEMCH had ceased to represent them.[7] However, all women's organizations participated in the *Jornada de Protesta Nacional* (Day for National Protest) called by the political parties and the *Comanda Nacional de Trabajadores* (National Workers Committee) on October 30, 1983.

In the atmosphere of polarization between the AD and MDP, women, not wanting the power of the masses to founder on the rocks of division, sought to unify the national opposition on the immediate goal at hand. Up to the middle of the year women participated in all the *Jornadas de Protesta* organized by political parties along with workers, unions and other youth groups. *Movimiento de Mujeres Socialistas*, highlighting the unity amongst all the opposition forces, came up with the slogan *Unidas por la Vida y la Libertad* (United for Life and Liberty).

In order to protest state censorship of the press and keep the flow of information going, a network of women who called themselves *Las Mensajeras* (the messengers) distributed editions of the *Movimiento Feminista* called *Hoja Informativa* (Information Page). With the slogan "Read, Multiply, Photocopy and Distribute," they managed to establish a flow of uncensored information.

The end of 1984 and the beginning of the following year witnessed intensive work amongst different women's groups to form the *Plataforma del MEMCH* in support of the United Nations' Convention on the Elimination of all Forms of Discrimination Against Women. Each women's group held forums and meetings that issued declarations which publicly denounced the Pinochet regime.

Mujeres por el Socialismo held a conference during which the *Coordinador Político de Mujeres de Oposición* was formed. On October 30, 1985, under the slogan of *Somos Más*, women formed different columns in the *Avenida Providencia* singing the national anthem and making public proclamations. They were joined by youths and professionals. A large number of protesters were detained and the demonstration was shown on television as a "subversive act." Nevertheless, women were once again demonstrating in Parque O'Higgins in November 1985 under the direction of the *Alianza Democrática* and the slogan *Chile Exige Democracia* (Chile Demands Democracy).

At the end of the year, *Mujeres por la Vida, Coordinador Político de Mujeres de Oposición*, MEMCH and MMS organized a massive demonstration with the slogan *86 es Nuestro - Palabra de Mujer* (1986 is Ours: Women's Word). Under the slogan *No Más Porque Somos Más* (No More Because We are More) women organized celebrations for the International Women's Day. On March 8, 1986, the International Day of Women, women sang that *Decimos No + Porque Somos* (We are saying No More, because we are more). They declared that they were saying no more to death, torture, exile, economic corruption, hunger, unemployment and a patriarchal dictatorship. The coordination of activities between the various groups continued to increase. On March 20, 1986, *Mujeres por la Vida* initiated a series of protests with the *Jornada por el Derecho a la Democracia* which were undertaken to demand a democratic government and the right to vote, to assemble and to go on strike.

We can conclude by saying that the women's movement in Chile manifested itself in different organizations having specific goals. The basic link between the three strands - feminists, human rights activists, and economic groups was that although their members came from different walks of life they were predominantly women. The basic goal that unified their actions was opposition to the military government and a desire for the return of democracy. Through intense mobilization and unity of the multiple organizations, the women's movement, in conjunction with the political parties, was able to pressure for an eventual transition to democracy in Chile.

Notes

[1] For a powerful analysis of the diversity of women's interests, see Maxine Molyneux, "Mobilization without Emancipation? Women's Interests, State, and Revolution," in *Transition and Development: Problems of Third World Socialism*, ed. Richard R. Fagen, Carmen Diana Deere, and José Luis Coraggio (New York: Monthly Review Press, 1986).

[2] Delsing categorizes these organizations on the basis of structure. Riet Delsing et al., *Tipologia de Organizaciones y Grupos de Mujeres Pobladoras*. Documento de Trabajo, No. 17 (Santiago: SUR, 1983).

[3] One should not take this to mean that women somehow completely escaped the repressions unleashed by the military government.

[4] For more information on the New Song Movement and the opposition of artists to the regime, see Nancy E. Morris, "Canto Porque es Necesario Cantar. The New Song Movement in Chile, 1973-1983," *Latin American Research Review* 21, no. 2 (1986).

[5] For more information regarding this angle, see Bernarda Gallardo, "El Redescubrimiento del Carácter Social del Hambre: Las Ollas Comunes," in *Espacio y Poder: Los Pobladores*, ed. Jorge Chateau et al (Santiago: FLACSO, 1987).

[6] For an excellent account of the daily lives of poor women in the urban shantytowns of Chile, see Teresa Valdés, *Venid, Benditas de mi Padre: Las Pobladoras, sus Rutinas y sus Sueños* (Santiago: FLACSO, 1988). See also Teresa Valdés, "Ser Mujer en Sectores Populares Urbanos" in *Espacio y Poder: Los Pobladores*, ed. Jorge Chateau (Santiago: FLACSO, 1987).

[7] The relationships between the AD and the MDP and their impact on women is discussed in Chapter four.

CHAPTER IV

The Women's Movement and the Rise of the Democratic Opposition

1983 is regarded as the year of protests and economic crisis in Chile. Earlier the economic shock and the neo-liberal experiment of the Chicago boys, the tearing down of trade barriers, the encouragement of free enterprise, and the reduction of state expenditure had meant a crisis for the poor. But the end of the so-called "Chilean economic miracle" in 1983–1984 entailed a crisis for the very same sectors of society that had promoted the coup and benefited from the military government's economic policies.[1]

Banks were virtually bankrupt, the external debt was rising, industrial production was paralyzed and unemployment was rampant. The neo-liberal model had contributed to greater impoverishment of the poorer sectors of society, and the promise of trickle-down for subsequent redistribution had not been met. Campero (1986) writes that the 1983 crisis should be considered as a "total" crisis for the regime: economic planning was slowly becoming politicized and the military's socio-cultural project was proving to be a disaster as well. The crisis for the regime was not only one of leadership but also marked the end of social consensus regarding the model of development that had been adopted by the military.

This period was also one of crisis for those opposing the military government (the political parties and the grass-roots organizations), due to their increasing inability to convene a unified opposition. The belief that political parties had been responsible for Chile's problems, the anti-party repression, and the "personalistic" politics introduced by Pinochet had led to the absence of intermediate actors and the demise of mediation and negotiation. Thus far, social movements had been acting without political parties serving as mediators between civil society and the state,[2] but now as political parties began to rebuild, the time was ripe for alliances and political alignments.

> One of the outstanding characteristics of Chilean politics in 1987–1988 is the return of political parties and their role as political representatives becoming more real than organizations such as the Church. (Alaminos 1989, 6)

Keeping in mind the pre-1973 history of the Chilean political parties, with their erosion during the repression of the early military period and their dramatic comeback, the obvious questions that arise are: What happened to the women's movement after the reestablishment of parties? Was it able to maintain its autonomy as a social movement, or did it get absorbed within the reconstruction process of the parties? What was the nature of the interaction between parties and the women's movement? Was the women's movement able to successfully convert its proposals addressing the subordination of women into concrete and powerful demands, and did political parties pay any attention to these demands? This chapter will seek to shed light on these questions.

Protest, Rejuvenation and Unified Opposition

By 1983, protests were not only possible in authoritarian Chile but had become essential for change; however, their success in radically altering the regime was extremely limited, even though they demonstrated the fact that the regime was faced with a "crisis of legitimacy." The regime answered the protests with increased repression rather than negotiation.[3] The whole experience of the protests and the breakdown of the National Accord (discussed later in this chapter) brought home the fact that the military government would agree only to an institutional transition, and the opposition was unable to come up with a solution that was agreeable to the military. This indicated the gap that existed between the ability to protest and the political strength necessary to propose a solution. In other words, there was a stark distinction between social actors at the base who were mobilizing and protesting and the national political actors (the political parties) with whom the military regime was willing to dialogue.[4] Pinochet was agreeable only to the solution laid down in the Constitution of 1980: a Presidential plebiscite in 1988 which would determine the future of the military government and of Chile.

During 1983, the political parties, regaining their vitality and membership, sought to unify the forces of opposition to the regime; however, this was easier said than done because of the crisis the Left was going through. The experiences of the coup and the subsequent repression and exile of members Communists and Socialists resulted in a breakdown of the alliance between the two parties. According to Oppenheim (1985), the Left then split into two distinct ideological camps: one, which advocated some form of bourgeois democracy with a mixed economy and the other, (made up of radical socialists, Communists and the MIR) which emphasized the necessity of violence in order to alter the existing situation. The efforts to obtain a unified opposition led to major regrouping and realignments. The upshot was the formation of two major blocs: the *Alianza Democrática*, or the Democratic Alliance (AD), a coalition of parties of the center-left, directed by the Christian Democratic Party (PDC), and the *Movimiento Democrático Popular*, or the Popular Democratic Movement (MDP), an alliance of extreme Left groups directed by the Communist Party (PC). The socialists were split, with a more moderate group in alliance with the Christian Democrats and another in the Communist bloc.[5]

The Democratic Alliance (AD) was of the opinion that mobilization should be used as a means of forcing the military government to engage in political dialogue and bargaining. The Popular Democratic Movement (MDP), on the other hand, was of the opinion that political mobilization was one of the strategies that could be used amongst other more radical forms of struggle. In its 1985 meeting, the PC recognized that there were two options available:

> In the opposition there are two basic projects ... one that favors a bourgeois-democratic exit from the dictatorship and the other that proposes a popular-democratic exit, with a view to socialism. (qtd. in Campero and Cortázar 1988, 117)

The military government, which interacted politically with the AD, granted it a "semi-institutional" status, while the MDP which advocated "all forms of struggle against the regime" fell into the realm of being "extrainsitutional" (Campero and Cortázar 1988). While the AD began to represent a credible opposition, the MDP became increasingly alienated; not only due to regime policies but also because of its unwillingness to enter into an alliance with the Christian Democrats. The Church, acting as peacemaker, initiated the National Accord between the AD and the military government represented by Sergio Onofre Jarpa, who was the Minister of the Interior. Although the Accord was a failure, it suggested that the removal of the military regime would be the result of a political settlement and not a "popular overthrow."

The AD's negotiations with the incipient "doves" in the military government during the *apertura* (opening) hinted that the government was inclined towards a negotiated political solution. The timetable for a peaceful transition was given in the Constitution of 1980 which established that there would be a plebiscite in 1988 to decide the fate of the military government. Chileans were presented with a choice between the continuation of the military government's model of development summarized in voting *Si* (yes), or a return to democracy denoted by voting for the alternative *No*. If the "No" prevailed, there would be presidential and parliamentary elections in 1989. If the "Yes" won, then Pinochet would be president for another eight years.

After the "National Protests" of 1984, the MDP called for a period of "Popular Protests" in which the AD and its adherents did not participate. Increased repression, lack of participation by all except the most radical and the absence of unity between the AD and the MDP led to increased demobilization of the masses until the calling of the *Asamblea de la Civilidad* (Assembly of Civility) in 1986. The Assembly provided social organizations and the political parties with an opportunity to articulate their demands at the national level. The women's movement was represented by María Antonieta Saa who presented the *Pliego de las Mujeres* (Specification of Women's Demands) to the Assembly. Prepared by *Mujeres por La Vida* and approved by other women's groups to be included in the *Pliego de Chile*, it called for respect for life, human rights and the dignity of all Chileans. It also articulated specific demands for the rights of women before the law, in education, in the family and in the workplace. Furthermore, it demanded measures that would ensure increased participation by women in all spheres of life and the ratification of the United Nations Convention on the Elimination of all Forms of Discrimination against Women.

Saa was arrested together with the other leaders of the Assembly. She declared from prison:

> We want democracy for Chile but also for ourselves. We want that our contribution be recognized and valued not only in words but also translated in our participation in social and political decision-making. We see democracy not only as a form of government but also as a way of life. We question all forms of authoritarianism. We have specific demands in the private and public life. (Cleary 1987, 271)

The importance of this event lies in the fact that women were seeking to define their role in a democratic Chile. The demands laid down very concretely the changes that women desired for themselves. The declaration was an attempt to carve a public space for women and make sure that their social participation would be converted into political representation.

Analysts of the democratic transition argue that political mobilization of various social organizations and movements led to the reconstruction of civil society, but it did not bring about the demise of the military government; the political parties and actors were indispensable in achieving that. Jelin (1987) proposes that the transition to democracy was a "political" or "institutional" period characterized by the dominance of political parties and political actors rather than social movements.[6] So the transition is essentially a political moment, and in Chile's case it was even more so because the agenda for transition was institutionalized by the military government in the Constitution of 1980 (which had been nationally accepted through a plebiscite).

The transition to democracy involved a dilemma for social movements in terms of their conversion from social actors into powerful political actors. How could these movements change the social strength of their organizations into political power? Touraine is of the opinion that the capacity to transform social actors into political actors is an indication of the level of democracy achieved in a nation. He writes that

> Democracy must be identified with the notion of representativity, above all. This notion presupposes not only the existence of representative institutions but also that of representable social actors, that is, of actors who are defined, organized, and capable of action before they have any channel of political representation. (Touraine 1988, 151)

In the initial phase of the military regime, social movements had been functioning as social actors that also undertook political roles. However, for the transition to democracy to become a reality, political parties and actors had to be revived, and the division of roles between the social and the political organizations had to be rearticulated. This meant that parties perform their time-honored role of representing the demands of groups in civil society and serve as mediators between state and society.

Political Parties and Social Movements

According to Garretón (1989a), political parties in Chile (prior to 1973) had been characterized by their stability, inclusion, representativeness, high level of ideologization and polarity, as well as by the immersion of social movements in the political parties. Chilean parties always absorbed within their structures and tended to establish corporatist relations with social movements. In order to gain access to an all-powerful state, one had to go through the all-pervasive political parties. The social movements, therefore, did not exist as independent entities. An example of a social movement's absorption by political parties in the pre-1973 period is the labor movement in Chile (Garretón 1989a; Muñoz 1987; Molina 1990).

The essential difference between the earlier social movements and the ones that arose under the dictatorship is that the latter were much more spontaneous and independent. According to Garretón,

> The autonomy of movements and social actors appears to be much greater in those new spaces that have opened up as part of the struggle against the military dictatorship: the human rights movement, the women's movement and other cultural movements. This is not to say that in all these movements' political party militants or leaders have not participated. But increasingly, these participants tend to define themselves more as militants of the respective movements and to disregard party directions. (1990d, 37)

The social movements now faced the dilemma of either establishing a relationship with the political parties on mutually acceptable terms and participating in the making of a new democratic state, or continuing to function solely in the realm of civil society. For the women's movement, the dilemma was a double-edged sword precisely because the political parties had previously not given priority to women's issues. Political parties have historically been male dominated spaces of power. Women have not enjoyed autonomous spaces in these institutions, which tended to relegate women into separate departments dealing with women's issues. Only during times of election, when the female vote was critical, did women's issues become important. Even worse, the Leftist parties had tended to subsume gender issues under the matrix of the class struggle without recognizing patriarchy as a form of discrimination and subordination quite distinct from class.

Thus, the first dilemma that the women's movement had to contend with was defining its strategy toward political parties: should it enter into alliances with parties in order to obtain access to the democratic political system that was being established or should it avoid the political realm and limit its goals to cultural change? Access to the political system could mean advancement in women's status in the democratic society that was being built; it could mean the support of the state in initiating change, as well the acceptance of gender issues as an integral part of the state's agenda. The debate that ensued within women's organizations revolved around two primary issues: (a) whether to define themselves as a "pure" social movement, working for change within society, or to enter into political alliances with the goal of gaining access to the political system as independent actors, and; (b) if political action was chosen, which of the two unified oppositions (AD or MDP) to join and on what terms?

The tensions in this debate created conflicts between the *políticas* (political militants) and the *feministas* (feminists). The conflict added another dimension to the earlier differences of class and gender discrimination which had divided the movement into supporters of the MDP and the AD. The *políticas* (who were members both of the feminist movement and political parties) wanted to work with the parties to end the dictatorship and establish a system that recognized the equality principle for both men and women. The *feministas*, on the other hand, feared the movement would lose its identity and autonomy, and would ultimately be subsumed by political parties (history would repeat itself) and nothing would be achieved. They argued that the movement should focus on initiating cultural change within society at large and the family in particular, not on gaining access to the political system. *Feministas* would rather have focused on changing the patriarchal relations that characterized society through consciousness-raising groups, seminars, workshops and the like. As far as politics was concerned, they claimed bipartisanship and did not fully trust the efficacy of reform legislation. The *políticas* retorted that given the legacy of strong political parties and the high levels of politicization and legalism in Chilean society, it would be difficult for the women's movement to accomplish its political demands outside of the purview of political parties.

It was strategy, not ideology that divided women's groups. The party militants emphasized the notion of power and the necessity for women to attain power and not be afraid of exercising it. They wanted equality within the political parties and greater access for women to positions of power in the party and the state. The *feministas*, on the other hand, were not desirous of power either in the party or the state. Though both groups of women were "feminist" in orientation, thought and spirit, their strategies adopted for bringing about change within the state and society were dramatically different.

The Wisdom in Strategizing

Women intellectuals writing on this issue highlighted the pros and cons of the positions in the debate. Molina and Serrano (1988) wrote that women could not hope to change into genuine political actors without a process of institutionalization that recognized them as such. As far as Chile was concerned, the history of the interaction between the women's movement and the state was not an "ideal" one to begin with. During the military dictatorship, the state had, in fact, been perceived as the "enemy," and had served the important function of uniting women against the regime. However, the administration that was to succeed the military government was not perceived as an enemy and, as it was a democratic one, it might even be a potential collaborator and "friend." According to Molina and Serrano, the time was ripe to negotiate and get the state to initiate change in favor of women. The important question they raised was whether women should marginalize themselves and stay peripheral to political power or join forces with the political parties and compete for positions in the government so as to influence policy making. Molina and Serrano noted the invaluable role of a "friendly" state in altering the political status of women but also emphasized the role of consciousness-raising groups in initiating cultural changes. They concluded by encouraging cooperation and coordination between women's organizations at the local, regional and national level, as well as between the *feministas* and the *políticas*.

The women's movement, if it did not wish to be completely excluded from politics and policy-making, had to strike a balance between interacting with political parties and the state on the one hand, and initiating cultural change within civil society and the family on the other. In a country like Chile, where political parties have been extremely strong, serving as a medium for pressuring the state, it was imperative that the women's movement collaborate with the political parties in order to initiate change in women's status. However, it was equally important to maintain the "autonomous" strand of the women's movement (the nonpartisan segment) which would be indispensable for putting pressure on parties and the state from without.

Most analysts of the Chilean transition are of the opinion that the role of social movements such as the *pobladoras* (shantytown dwellers) and the syndicates in the transition to democracy was determined largely by their relation, interaction and interdependence with political parties.[7] In this sense, the women's movement was no different; it was essential to strike a balance between being politically effective and enjoying a considerable amount of autonomy as a social movement. The challenge for the women's movement was how to express itself at the political level, have an impact in the political arena and guarantee a space for itself in national politics, but at the same time, guard its autonomy and grass-root base and avoid co-optation by "malestream" politics. It was imperative to prevent both the state and the political parties from subsuming the social movements.

Eventually, the women's movement was successfully able to transform social participation, mobilization and visibility into political representation and strength. Most social movements that flourished under the dictatorship were unable to make this essential transition. The united efforts of the party militants and the *feministas* help explain the success of the women's movement. The *políticas*' ability to pressure the parties to accept their demands and recognize their contributions was important.

Also important was the critique of patriarchy which was specific to the movement. Experiences with authoritarianism in women's daily lives, both in the family and in the nation, helped them identify the system they wished to change. Patriarchy, with its division of roles between the sexes and between the private and the public realm, helped women make the argument that with the return of "politics as usual" women would be prevented from entering the public sphere. This argument appealed to the political elites, whose desire to eliminate marginality and divisiveness led them to initiate changes to improve the status of women. Thus, the *políticas* and *feministas* found willing allies in the political elites who took up their cause of gender equality during the transition to democracy. Therefore, at least for the time being, a fruitful and win-win situation was achieved between the political parties and the women's movement.

Once the decision was made to cooperate whole-heartedly with the political parties for establishing democracy and introducing women's issues in the agenda of the political parties and the state, a second decision had to be reached to determine which opposition group (the MDP or the AD) to join. The inability of the AD and MDP to iron out their differences and elaborate a unified political alternative had an impact on the women's movement. Characterized by the participation of lower and middle-class women, professionals and housewives, and militants of the Center and the Left, the women's movement was striving to be both multi-class and ideologically pluralistic. With the return of the political parties, the political affiliations of the women became more overt, and members of the movement began to be subjected to the alignments and alliances of their respective political parties. The radical group of the women's movement (mostly lower-class women who were a part of MEMCH) went with the MDP, while the bulk of the upper lower-class and the middle-class joined the AD. The differences between the political parties crept into the movement's agenda and interfered with its unity. It was not so much a conflict between the women as between the leadership and the strategies of the political parties that invariably made its way into the rank and file of the women's movement. Thus, the PDC did not "permit" its female party militants to participate and support the activities of MEMCH, since that organization was inextricably aligned with the political tendencies of the extreme left who were not a part of the AD.[8] On the other hand, the extreme Left parties did not wish to participate in the plebiscite or the election. Since they did not recognize the legitimacy of the 1980 Constitution, they refused to play by the rules established by a regime and a constitution they considered neither legal nor representative of the nation. Eventually, they participated in both but at the cost of considerable confusion amongst their rank and file with miscommunication that harmed them electorally and caused conflict for the women's movement.

In conclusion, the period of the transition witnessed a change in the actions and goals of several women's groups in particular and the movement in general. Initially, the movement's goal was opposition to the military regime and the creation of a space to manifest this opposition. At that time, the very existence of these spaces of opposition and protest amounted to resistance. During the period of the *apertura* (opening), when the transition to democracy and the establishment of a civilian government became a reality, women's groups expressed specific demands. While it was politically astute to raise issues specific to women as a distinct social group, the immediate goal was a return to democracy. Women's groups were now involved in "political" activity as they presented demands and proposals to the parties with the hope of winning substantial concessions in return. They engaged in negotiations and collaborations in the hope of ultimately carving a space for women in the national political sphere. For the most part, the various women's groups were able to underplay their differences in order to push for an improvement in women's status.

Women, Political Parties and "No"

Since it had become clear that the only way to initiate democracy was to beat the military government at its own game, in accordance with the framework laid down in the 1980 Constitution, the political parties realized that the entire struggle for democracy should revolve around the regime's defeat in the plebiscite. Consequently they set out to work intensively on encouraging voter registration. The women's movement had realized as well that it would be more practical to work with the AD since the establishment of democracy and the removal of the military regime was an essential prerequisite for any kind of improvement in women's situations.

Thus, the goal was very clear: cooperate and focus on defeating Pinochet. Unity and cooperation could achieve democracy which in turn would provide a platform for women's demands. The subordination of women's goals to the struggle for democracy was dictated by pragmatism. What was essential was the strengthening of networks and a focus on action. This realization led to the rise of a group named *Mujeres por la Democracia* (Women for Democracy) which called for a smooth and non-violent transition to democracy.[9] This group consisted of housewives and women from political parties, universities, labor associations, social and political organizations and Christian Base Communities.

The *Comando Mujeres por el No* (Women's Command for "No") consisting of representatives of political parties, social and political organizations as well as various sectors of society came into being and focused on projecting an image of unity against the military government. The highest organ of the *Comando* (Command) was called the *Comité de Personalidades* (Committee of Personalities), a group of high-profile, well-known women of diverse political tendencies who projected the public image of the *Comando* and participated in events, meetings and conventions, visiting different provinces and regions. A *Coordinación Política* (Political Coordinator) was responsible for planning and coordinating the actions of the third organ, called *Comisiones* (Commissions), made up of representatives of various political parties and technical organizations. The *Comando* had branches in various zones and regions not only in Santiago but throughout the nation. Slogans, such as *Porque somos Más, Las Mujeres Votamos No* (Since We are More Numerous, Women Vote No), were the order of the day. The militants of the PDC were instrumental in forming a group called *Mujeres Integradas por Elecciones Libres*, or Women United for Free Elections (MIEL). Women of distinct political tendencies, housewives, professionals, *campesinas* and intellectuals, realizing their heterogeneity but at the same time emphasizing their pluralism and quest for democracy, came together to demand free, fair and competitive elections in Chile.

Another organization, *Mujeres Unidas por el NO* (Women United for "No") was formed in March 1988. This group consisted of women from the PDC, Socialist, Humanist, Green, Radical, and the Christian Left parties (all the parties that came together in 1988 to form a *Concertación* or Coalition to promote a "No" vote). In their pamphlets, women listed ten different reasons urging people to vote "No" in the forthcoming plebiscite. Their pamphlets advocated saying "No" to the dictatorship, to violence, to a culture of death, to social injustice, to abuse of power and to repression. According to them, casting a "No" vote was essential for regaining people's lost sovereignty, respect for human rights, peace and tranquility in the country.

Concertación Nacional de Mujeres por la Democracia (CNMD)

As a result of the victory in the Plebiscite of the "No" organizations, on December 16, 1988, an extremely important women's organization came into being: the *Concertación Nacional de Mujeres por la Democracia* (National Coalition of Women for Democracy—CNMD). It consisted predominantly of women who were party militants although there were some independent feminists as well. The *Concertación* contributed to the Presidential and parliamentary campaigns, maintained national attention on women's rights and encouraged women's participation in the struggle for democracy. It is important to understand that the *Concertación Nacional de Mujeres por la Democracia* consisted to a large extent of the female militants of parties that were a part of the *Concertación de Partidos por el No* (Coalition of Parties for No). The *Concertación de Partidos por el No* (during the Plebiscite) became the *Concertación de Partidos por la Democracia* (Coalition of Parties for Democracy) for the election. The extreme left was not a part of this *Concertación*. The CNMD was therefore an initiative of the political parties and the *políticas* to ensure the inclusion of the "Woman Question" into the program of the *Concertación*.

The *Concertación* was created in Santiago and in the major cities in the provinces in order to encourage coordination of women's activities. However, in the provinces, it was mainly political party militants who participated. In Santiago itself, around 150 women took part in the *Concertación* which was directed by both a Council and an Operations Committee. Four major Working Commissions focused on building a Program, Presence of Women in Public Life, Mobilization, and Art and Culture. The *Concertación* set up eleven commissions of experts in order to investigate the situation of women in the fields of education, health, family, communications, art and culture, employment, the peasantry, the shantytown dwellers, political participation legislation and the national office for women.[10] These commissions worked autonomously and consisted of women who were members of the CNMD and considered experts on the topics under discussion.

The findings and suggestions provided by these commissions served as the foundation of the program for women of the *Concertación de Partidos por la Democracia* (Coalition of Parties for Democracy) which formed the unified opposition to Pinochet in the Plebiscite. After winning the Plebiscite, this Coalition went on to compete in the Presidential and Parliamentary elections that followed. So the *Concertación* played an extremely important role in making women's issues part of the national scene, formulating a program for women in the future democratic government and working in the upcoming presidential election (Montecino and Rossetti 1990, 7). It promoted women in politics, public administration and local government, and brought national attention to women's problems through declarations and conferences. The *Concertación* also elaborated a list of possible female candidates who were committed to women's issues. The CNMD's main focus was to win the highest number of votes for the candidates of the *Concertación de Partidos por la Democracia*. It sought to spread the idea that women had rights, that they were discriminated against and that a government program should be established for attaining equality between men and women.[11] The CNMD's work was extremely important in dispelling the notion of women's support for the military coup as well as stereotypes about women's conservative political tendencies. The CNMD had to work long and hard in order to emphasize the importance of the feminine vote for the victory of democracy. In spite of not having complete and free access to the media, the CNMD achieved its goals through networks and workshops as well as discussion groups. Emphasis was laid on the inherent value of democracy, the proposals of the CNMD regarding women and the program of the *Concertación de Partidos*. On August 20, 1989, the CNMD organized a massive convention in Caupolicán (attended by five thousand women) where Patricio Aylwin, the Coalition's presidential candidate, announced his government's policy towards women. In January 1990, after the election, the CNMD issued a report that outlined its activities, findings and programs regarding women. After the CNMD was formally dissolved, the female members of the parties of the *Concertación* did meet once again in August 1990 to discuss the democratic government's policies in different spheres and to outline the problems that confronted women in the 1990s.[12]

The *Coordinación de Organizaciones Sociales de Mujeres* (Coordination of Women's Social Organizations) initiated a project of their own. They felt that the needs and demands of popular class women were not being sufficiently addressed by the CNMD and its eleven commissions since no lower-class women were represented on these panels. According to them, the CNMD's suggestions were colored by the political affiliations of women on these panels who were mostly party militants. The Coordination wanted to undertake a study that would be independent of the political parties and would represent the needs of women's social organizations rather than those of party militants.[13] Consequently, professionals from academic institutions, such as the *Facultad Latinoamericana de Ciencias Sociales* (FLACSO), the *Servicio Evangélico para el Desarrollo* (SEPADE) and a team of training experts from MEMCH'83 worked with base organizations from different sectors of Santiago for a period of five months. This was also part of a campaign initiated by the *Coordinacion de Organizaciones Sociales de Mujeres* called *Soy Mujer ... Tengo Derechos* (I Am a Woman and I Have Rights) in June 1989. A series of *jornadas* (working days) were set up where common problems were shared and discussed. Out of these emerged demands for change and proposals for action affecting popular women in particular.

The "Wooing" of Women

After the plebiscite, women began to put pressure on their parties to eliminate the *Departamento Femeninos* (Women's Departments) which were nothing more than ghettos for women; they demanded the inclusion of women within the higher echelons of political parties. An important victory in this direction was the introduction of positive discrimination in the *Partido por la Democracia*, or the PPD. After the triumph of the "No," the PPD initiated an internal democratization process, approving a rule of guaranteeing representation to women in at least twenty percent of all party positions. It is worth noting that this served only as a minimum guideline and there could be more women, but not less. The PPD was the first political party in Chile to introduce this innovative and progressive norm in its internal regulations. It was followed by the Radical party. The PDC has not adopted a similar measure, but members of the *Technico* (Department) have been pressuring for the inclusion of more female candidates in party lists. The *Humanistas-Verdes* did not have a *Departamento Femenino* or positive discrimination.

Critics of positive discrimination have denounced the measure, saying that it does not affect women at the lower rungs and leads to the concentration of benefits for certain women. Proponents respond by declaring that it has contributed to greater representation of women at the lower levels of leadership and that fifty percent of the leadership positions in the PPD are, in fact, being held by women. The introduction of positive discrimination was one attempt to restructure power relations in political parties. Most women party militants perceived it as a precedent that could go a long way in eliminating inherent mechanisms of discrimination and encourage women to attain valuable leadership experience. It was also seen as an effective measure to promote and facilitate the election of female candidates to Parliament.

The presence and participation of women in political parties was on the increase in the late 1980s. Fifty-two percent of the national electorate is female and 51.2 percent of the women voters voted "No" in the plebiscite (Hirmas and Gomariz 1990, 21). In some parties, such as the PPD and the *Humanistas*, half of the party militants were women. The increasing political participation of women can be explained in terms of their experience of the dictatorship and the massive mobilization of women as "citizens" and opponents of the regime, as well as the realization by political parties that they must increase the representation and participation of women in every sphere of society if a genuine participatory democracy is to be established. If women continued to feel excluded then the efforts to deepen democratic reconstruction would be rendered futile. A definite, progressive policy towards women was essential.

The participants in the election of 1990 were the Right (UDI and PRN), the *Concertación* (Center-Left coalition) and the Communists. The *Concertación* came up with one presidential candidate, Patricio Aylwin, and the right with two, Hernán Buchi and Francisco J. Errázuriz. The *Concertación* issued a pamphlet which declared "Women shine by their absence in Buchi's program." Buchi's campaign reiterated women's traditional roles as mothers and housewives. He was accused of proposing a superficial and conservative role for women, and it was pointed out that "Women's Rights" was the last issue to be covered in his program.

Patricio Aylwin, on the other hand, was in constant contact with the women's organizations and had presented an extremely attractive and powerful program for women in a public speech in Caupolicán Theater on August 20, 1989. The *Concertación* declared that it would create family tribunals, come up with programs to assist abandoned and separated families, and make the rights of illegitimate children similar to those of legitimate ones. It was also quick to point out that it sought to strengthen the family from the point of view of increasing the rights of women. Child care was not just a woman's responsibility the father must do his share as well. More profoundly, the *Concertación* would pass legislation regarding domestic violence, equal rights over children, and establish equality between men and women. Thus concerted efforts were being made to woo the feminine vote. The *Concertación* also initiated a program called *Mujer Chile Te Quiere* (Woman, Chile Wants You), in which a series of workshops were held to encourage reflection and suggestions regarding the building of a new and democratic Chile. Women from all walks of life met in their parties, social and political organizations and workshops, to talk about the community, the family and work. After identifying the problems they confronted in each of these areas, they came up with possible solutions. At the end there was a huge convention in Valparaiso where delegates from various groups presented feedback.

The *Concertación* expressed its political will to listen to women and support their demands with the goal of building political democracy. Molina (1989a), writing about three aspects of Aylwin's speech at Caupolican that merited discussion, concluded that Aylwin clearly understood that national problems affected women and men in different ways and, therefore, it was necessary for legislators to consider women as a disparate group. Second, he realized that for cultural reasons, certain aspects of life such as childcare, domestic violence and job discrimination affected women more than men. In this regard, Aylwin elaborated a vision of public policy which was unprecedented in its consideration of the gender issue. Third, he promised to create a state agency to coordinate public policies catering to the needs of women and stimulating women's participation in national life (Molina 1989a).

The ability of the *Concertación* to come up with a program including women's demands showed that the new government wanted to involve all Chileans in the transition to democracy, and avoid at all costs the national problems caused by the exclusion of certain sectors of society. The *Concertación* seemed to understand the difference between political and social democratization. The former demands women's cooperation with the state and formal political structures which formulate public policies while the latter requires a strong social movement targeting cultural change in the family and other social structures.[14]

The *Concertación*'s willingness to create a space for women ensured that society as a whole would assume responsibility for meeting women's demands. The fact that a new "space" was provided for women did not imply the absorption of the movement by the state or the political parties; rather, it amounted to the creation of a mechanism that would channel the demands of women and civil society to the state, making sure that public policies were sensitive to gender issues.

Courting the Human Rights Lobby and the *Pobladora*

On September 28, 1988, during the campaign preceding the Plebiscite, a huge demonstration for the defense of human rights was held in the Municipal Stadium of Melipilla. The *Agrupación de Familiares de Detenidos y Desaparecidos* (AFDD) also participated in an Amnesty International Concert held in the National Stadium on October 12 and 13, 1990.[15] The human rights organizations (primarily made up of women) had participated on a regular basis in demonstrations against the military government. As has already been mentioned, women, through their constant protests, were able to make respect for human rights an integral part of the Chilean political culture. In order for human rights to continue to be an important issue in Chile, it was essential that the human rights groups enter into some alliances with the potential government.

A public commitment was signed by the political parties of the Left and the *Humanista-Verde* on August 12, 1988. They demanded an annulment of the effects and extensions of the Law of Amnesty (D.L.2.191), passed in 1978, which did not permit the events that occurred between September 11, 1973 and March 10, 1978 to be opened for investigation in a court of law. The declaration asked the Tribunals to fulfill their functions in accordance with the principles of truth and justice and punish those who were responsible for the crimes, and promise that no further laws of impunity would be accepted. The political parties also promised to elaborate a plan specifying reparations for the victims and their families and initiate legislation that would declare detention-disappearance a crime against humanity. The AFDD signed this petition making a commitment *Por la Verdad y la Justicia* (For Truth and Justice) and declaring *No a la Impunidad* ("No" to Impunity).

The *Concertación* did not spell a radical change from the military regime's economic policies, but it promised to promote social justice and to increase social expenditure. This amounted to an acknowledgement of the failure of military government's model of development. The *Concertación* did not advocate a complete reversal of economic policy but it did propose a comparatively greater role for the state in the distribution of goods and services rather than absolute dependence on market forces. With the return of a democratic system, the state sought to intervene in promoting social justice and creating a social net for the popular classes through increased expenditure. It achieved this through the creation of the *Fondo de Solidaridad y Inversión Social* (FOSIS) which was a part of ODEPLAN (Ministry of Planning and Cooperation). FOSIS sought to resolve the most urgent problems of the poor sectors of society.[16]

In conclusion, the women's movement in Chile was successful in converting itself from a social actor to a political actor. It was able to do this due to the organizational diversity of the movement and the unity these disparate groups maintained to achieve political ends. No one strand of the movement was more powerful than the other, and precisely because of this, the movement was able to deal with the challenges that it faced. If human rights groups had been stronger than other women's groups or if the women's movement was made up only of human rights activists, it might not have had the political clout necessary to negotiate with parties and raise important issues. If only the *feministas* had constituted the women's movement in Chile, they would probably have focused on cultural change and building civil society which would have translated into political isolation once political parties came to power. If they had continued to engage in autonomous activity without entering into alliances with the parties or the state, they would have severely limited their power to convert women's demands into legislation. If, on the other hand, the *políticas* had independently dominated the women's movement in Chile, the political parties would likely have been able to override women's demands once again in the name of national exigencies and priorities.

As we have seen in this chapter, Chilean women were able to utilize effectively the diversity of the women's movement to pursue multiple strategies, create various avenues for negotiation and pressure different points not only to gain access to the public sphere but also to publicize the gender issue in political parties, the state, and society at large.

Notes

1. For more details on these economic aspects, see Alejandro Foxley, "The Neoconservative Economic Experiment in Chile;" and Pilar Vergara, "Changes in the Economic Functions of the Chilean State under the Military Regime," both in *Military Rule in Chile. Dictatorship and Oppositions*, ed. J. Samuel Valenzuela and Arturo Valenzuela (Baltimore: Johns Hopkins University Press, 1986).

2. Rodrigo Baño makes a similar point in an expose titled "La Relación entre Partidos y Movimiento Sociales," in *Lo Social y Lo Político, Un Dilema Clave del Movimiento Popular* (Santiago: FLACSO, 1985).

3. For information regarding the increased repression of the military regime, see Guillermo Campero and René Cortázar, "Actores Sociales y la Transición a la Democracia en Chile," in *Estudios CIEPLAN*, No. 25 (Santiago: CIEPLAN, 1988). Campero and Cortázar write that cases of torture registered with the *Vicaria* declined in half between 1980-82. However, after the beginning of the period of mobilization (1984-86), political repression heightened. Cases of torture increased by more than fifty percent in comparison to figures of the 1980-82 period. The number of deaths caused by state repression almost quintupled.

4. For detailed information on these protests see Mario Garcés and Gonzalo de la Maza, *La Explosión de las Mayorías. Protesta Nacional 1983-1984* (Santiago: ECO, 1985).

5. For more on this see Lois Oppenheim, "Democracy and Social Transformation: The Debate within the Left," *Latin American Perspectives* 46, no. 3 (1985): 59-76.

6. For a detailed exposition of this argument see Elizabeth Jelin, "El Itinerario de la Democratización, los Movimientos Sociales y la Participación Popular," in *Marginalidad, Movimientos Sociales y Democracia*. Proposiciones, No. 14 (Santiago: SUR, 1987). See also Manuel A. Garretón, "Las Complejidades de la Transición Invisible. Movilizaciones Populares y Régimen Militar en Chile," in *Marginalidad, Movimientos Sociales y Democracia*. Proposiciones, No. 14 (Santiago: SUR, 1987).

7. For a further discussion of this relation see Campero and Cortázar, "Actores Sociales y la Transición a la Democracia en Chile."

8. Information obtained through interviews with members of MEMCH, the PDC as well as other organizations.

[9.] All the information on women's work and organizations set up during the plebiscite is based on interviews and on the personal pamphlets, working papers and documents made available by Mariana Aywlin who granted me access to her personal archives.

[10.] For information on the findings and suggestions of these commissions, see Sonia Montecino and Josefina Rossetti, eds., *Tramas para un Nuevo Destino: Propuestas de la Concertación de Mujeres por la Democracia* (Santiago, 1990).

[11.] Interviews with participants of the *Concertación de Mujeres por la Democracia*.

[12.] The results and discussions of this meeting can be found in Josefina Rossetti, ed., *Ideas para la Acción: Encuentro de la Concertración de Mujeres por la Democracia* (Santiago, 1991).

[13.] Interviews with members of MEMCH, RIDEM and other organizations as well as independent feminists who participated in the project.

[14.] For more on this issue see Lilian Mires, Natacha Molina, and M. E. Valenzuela, *Cambio Social, Transición y Políticas Públicas Hacia la Mujer*. Paper presented at the Seminario Internacional Cambio Social, Transición y Políticas Publicas Hacia la Mujer. Santiago, Sept. 1989.

[15.] Information obtained from *Luchando Unidos Encontraremos la Verdad, Reseña Histórica del Conjunto Folclorico de la Agrupación de Familiares de Detenidos-Desaparecidos* and *IX Semana Internacional por los Detenidos y Desaparecidos* (Santiago: AFDD, Vicaría de la Solidaridad). The issue of redress and reparation for past human rights violations is updated in Chapter five.

[16.] The next chapter will deal with this issue at length.

CHAPTER V

Women, the State and Civil Society

It became clear in the last chapter that the women's movement in Chile was successful in transforming itself into a political force while maintaining its cultural dimension due to the differences in strategies between the *políticas* and the *feministas*. The first part of this chapter will show how the women's movement successfully continues to compel the State and political elites to recognize and address discrimination and oppression against women. The latter half of the chapter will focus on the shape that the movement attained in civil society and how the work in which women's organizations engage "maintains" the movement.

Scholars of social movements argue that they essentially struggle for increased democratization of society (Offe 1987; Habermas 1981; Touraine 1981, 1983, 1987; Evers 1985; and Cohen 1983). Melucci writes that social movements force "the ruling groups to innovate, to permit changes among elites, to admit what was previously excluded from the decision-making arena and to expose the shadowy zones of power" (1988, 255). The specific strategic goals of the women's movement in Chile could have been achieved only with the help of reform-oriented parties and elites within the political system. The women's movement aimed towards democratization of the State and society, but it needed political power to transform these demands into action. This capacity was provided through successful negotiations with the political parties and the *Concertación* that eventually constituted the state.

So, what happened to the women's movement in Chile after the transition to democracy? It continued to exist but had to adapt itself to a new reality. The ability to adopt new forms and structures in changing circumstances is another characteristic of a successful social movement. Restructuring is intricately tied up to a movement's continued existence, and movements which are unable to restructure may become exhausted and disappear. Some writers contend that the women's movement in Chile lacks a single, unified and centralized organization with commonly established goals and broadly accepted strategies for action, and that the absence of these characteristics leads to the diffusion and fragmentation of women's energies and mobilization. But one could argue that this decentralization is itself an important characteristic of any movement.

Melucci writes that "what empirically is called a social movement is a system of action, connecting plural orientations and meanings. A single collective action ... contains different kinds of behavior" (1985, 794). It seems that in Chile today, a women's movement exists, inside the state, political parties and in civil society. In civil society, diverse women's organizations have adopted the form of a "community" in order to meet the needs of the day. What was earlier a dense network of women with no formal structures is now a multitude of formal, structured organizations that have adopted different strategies for initiating social change.

> The normal situation of today's movement is to be a network of small groups submerged in everyday life which requires a personal involvement in experiencing and practicing cultural innovation. They emerge only on specific issues. (Melucci 1984, 829)

The movement consists of a network of groups sharing common goals and values. This is no different from the definition that Zald gives to a social movement industry (McCarthy and Zald, 1977). In the post-military period, there are no women protesting out in the streets. Though the old forms of protest and mobilization are missing, this is a natural consequence of the state no longer being the overt enemy that it was under the military regime. As McCamant (1989) writes, when the nature, dynamic and the form of domination change radically, a corresponding change occurs in the form and nature of the resistance and opposition. The state is no longer the "opposition:" the rules of the game demand that the women's movement develop ways of cooperating and negotiating with traditional actors. The movement must maintain a working relation with those in power in order to implement the advantages it has won and pressure for new gender-sensitive changes in legislation and public policies. So while the movement may be overtly demobilized, it is hardly dead.

Women and a "Gender-Responsive" State

The new democratic state satisfied some of the demands made by women by setting up the *Servicio Nacional de la Mujer* (SERNAM) or the "National Service for Women." The *Concertación de Mujeres por la Democracia* thought it necessary to push for the creation of a National Office for Women to promote genuine consciousness of gender issues and stimulate public policy initiatives to improve the reality of Chilean women. The *políticas* demanded a ministry of this kind to guarantee that women would not only be represented in the State, but also encouraged to participate in the country's social, economic, political and cultural development. The Right (UDI and PRN) opposed the formation of SERNAM on the grounds that it would be a "Ministry of Feminists," through which the state would try to control and manipulate the private sphere. The Right also feared that the Left would utilize SERNAM to infiltrate women's groups and ruin the Chilean family system. But with the passage of Law No. 19.023 on 3 January 1991, SERNAM officially came into being as state agency with ministerial rank. It is essentially reformist in spirit, engaging in lobbying activities necessary to convert women's needs and demands into legislative and public policy issues. SERNAM has no independent executive and financial powers, and it works with different ministries, municipalities, NGOs and women's organizations to encourage women's participation in national life and propose gender-oriented legislation.[1]

While SERNAM is not a ministry on its own, it is a part of the Ministry of Planning and Cooperation (MIDEPLAN), this organization is responsible for social programs in Chile. The other portions of MIDEPLAN focus on marginalized persons within Chile; for example, those who are indigenous and poverty stricken. These programs generally are not executing policy, rather they are designing policy and funding for social organizations and NGO's to run (Franceshet, 2003). In some ways this position for SERNAM is both weakening and empowering. Had SERNAM become a separated entity, it would likely have turned into a ghetto for an issue that other ministries did not need to deal with. However, the director of SERNAM is a ranking minister of state, thus she has participation in cabinet meetings and has the power of position within the ministry (Franceshet, 2003).

María Soledad Alvear was SERNAM's first Director and the only woman member of Aylwin's Cabinet. The current director is Cecilia Pérez. SERNAM has a total of fifty-nine professionals working for it and a regional, decentralized structure; it works through thirteen Regional offices responsible for implementing its agenda at the provincial and community level.[2] Some of the goals established at SERNAM's formation had been achieved by the end of Aylwin's four years in office. SERNAM worked with the Ministry of Labor to reform the Labor Code by eliminating articles that excluded women from certain jobs and by establishing rights for temporary and domestic workers. The reform also included increased parental rights for workers and a proposal to reform the Civil Code to empower married women to independently administer their own estate is being discussed as an acceptable alternative to the existing law. SERNAM has also been successful in establishing Centers of Information regarding women's rights and the resources available to women throughout the country. It successfully launched a program for assisting female heads of households with the cooperation of the Municipality of Santiago, and it was instrumental in passing a law making domestic violence a crime against women.[3] In addition to these successes, SERNAM has introduced legislation protecting women from job loss, providing healthcare to temporary workers, increasing women's rights within families, and protecting pregnant teenagers from being expelled from schools (Francechet 2003).

SERNAM has recently organized a *plan de igualidad entre mujeres y hombres* (Plan for equality between women and men). This plan includes goals to be reached by the year 2010, which were put into action starting in 2000. Goals of the plan include creating a bad image of gender discrimination, eliminating stereotypes of gender, adding gender to educational curriculum, fomenting knowledge and artistry that take into account the differences between genders, and promoting and guaranteeing the rights of women. The plan is also specified for every region in addition to an overall plan for the country (*Plan de Igualidad entre Mujeres y Hombres,* January 2000). This plan has the potential to change the face of Chilean Feminism.

However, some of SERNAM's proposals have met with defeat, notably an attempt to include an equal rights amendment in the Constitution. Furthermore, some especially divisive issues have not yet been tackled by the agency, including contraception, abortion and divorce. During the Aylwin administration, Adriana Muñoz, member of the PPD and a Deputy in Parliament, introduced a bill pressing for the legalization of therapeutic abortion. Seminars and discussions on divorce are held on a regular basis and Laura Rodriguez of the *HV* party has even introduced legislation in Congress. There continues to be a great deal of discussion on these issues but no change in legislation so far. SERNAM defends its neutral position by claiming that it is a technical office which is not permitted to intervene in the moral issues of society and, therefore, cannot initiate legislation on either divorce or abortion. SERNAM's emphasis on moderation and avoiding conflict, together with the overwhelming influence of the Catholic Church, which does not support any of these issues, has resulted in the maintenance of the status quo for several women's issues.[4]

SERNAM's list of achievements is fairly long and impressive, but the agency has not been spared criticism by the women's movement and political parties. Some feminists argue that through SERNAM the women's movement and its agenda have been co-opted by the state. Elisabeth Friedman claims that state women's agencies are "powerless without a corresponding mass movement of the social sector [they are] established to represent" (qtd. in Franceschet, 2003: 17). Others contend that women's organizations in civil society have suffered from a lack of good leadership since many professional women left these autonomous organizations to work in SERNAM. Still others believe that few women holding top positions in SERNAM are committed feminists or experienced activists from women's organizations. Some women's organizations find SERNAM's discourse too conservative, and so they distance themselves completely from it, contending that the agency does not speak for them. Another alleged shortcoming of SERNAM is that its discourse seems to focus more on women in terms of the family rather than just women themselves. As Chuchryk writes,

> Unfortunately, SERNAM has replaced the women's movement as the key interlocutor in the public discourse on women's issues. It is a government agency that consistently frames women's issues in the context of the need to preserve and harmonize family life. (1994, 88)

But SERNAM, undoubtedly, has been successful in including women's issues in the democratic government's agenda. Soledad Larrain declared that (through SERNAM) the state has taken steps to include women not only as "objects" of policies but also "active subjects" of policies. Innumerable inequalities confronting women can be rectified through public policy, and SERNAM, despite several inherent shortcomings in its structure, exhibits a great deal of initiative. It enjoys a national presence and has utilized its proximity to nationally powerful male elites to become an institution which presents women's demands to an androcentric state.[5] It is the only agency in the government that has consistently sought to place women at the center of policy-making. SERNAM has to move cautiously and slowly given the criticism of the Right and the influence of Catholicism. Moreover, it does not enjoy complete financial or political autonomy and, thus, does not have the political muscle to implement all its programs.

While in most cases women's movements have weakened in Latin America with the change to democracy, conversely, it seems that the Chilean women's movement has grown stronger on the whole, which can for a large part be attributed to SERNAM. In the climate of the neoliberal model most social services and provisions have been withdrawn from governmental organization. However, with SERNAM as a pillar in the state, an environment can still be fostered for women's activism. The ministry also provides the function of separating the women's movement from entrenchment in party politics. From its position in the state, SERNAM is able to conduct the relations between several different women's groups throughout Chile (Franceschet 2003).

Along these lines, SERNAM has coordinated with *el Proceso Consulta Nacional de Consultas Indigenas* (CONADI), "the national process of indigenous questions", and with PRODEMU an agency for promotion and development of women in order to set up *Mesas de la Mujer Indigena*, or "Tables of indigenous women". These initiatives allow small groups of indigenous women to group together in order to improve their lifestyle; they learn practical and personal skills while building self-confidence together. Also, joining forces with CONADI, SERNAM has produced legislation improving the healthcare and social standing of *trabajadoras temporales* or "temporary workers", who are generally indigenous and living in extreme poverty with no real certainty or security with regard to their financial standing (Interview with Pilar Fica, Coordinator of PRODEMU Canete, May 7, 2003). In addition, several women's organizations on a more local level are forming cooperatives with the agricultural and economic advice of INDAP *Instituto Nacional de Desarrolo Agropecuaro* (national institute for agricultural development) and SERNAM; these cooperatives provide women an excellent opportunity to create connections and development to improve their own lives (Interview with Pilar Fica, Coordinator of PRODEMU Cañete, May 7, 2003).

Another women's agency that has grown under the auspices of the democratic regime is *Promoción y Desarrollo de la Mujer*, or "Promotion and Development of Women" (PRODEMU), created by the Aylwin administration in November 1990 to support grass-roots women's organizations. While SERNAM operates primarily at the national level, PRODEMU works more at the local level and with women's organizations existing at the base. Whereas SERNAM seeks to make public policies more sensitive to gender issues, the primary function of PRODEMU is to support and empower autonomous women's organizations, especially the *Centros de Madres* and the *talleres*.

PRODEMU was established under the Presidency of the First Lady and it serves all Chilean women irrespective of ideology, religion or social standing; however, its work normally revolves around groups and organizations of women with limited resources. It offers direct assistance through workshops focusing on personal development, civic growth, improvement of quality of life and cultural values. It serves as a source of information regarding programs and policies benefiting women, and coordinates the efforts of governmental and non-governmental institutions wishing to support women.[6]

No! a la Impunidad: Women and Human Rights

While seeking to win female support and emphasize its commitment to democracy, the incoming government also sought to render justice to the human rights groups which constituted another segment of the women's movement. In keeping with the accord signed between the various human rights organizations and the *Concertación* on April 24, 1990, President Patricio Aylwin created (through a special presidential decree) the "National Commission on Truth and Reconciliation." The Commission's objective was to investigate the massive human rights violations that transpired during the dictatorship and to suggest ways of national reconciliation. The Commission, headed by Raul Rettig Guissen, consisted of eight members two of which were women. The Rettig Commission was in no way empowered to guarantee that justice would be done - that responsibility lay with the courts alone - but human rights groups did present their demands for "Truth and Justice" to the Commission. The groups suggested measures through which reparations could be made to victims of the repression and their families: via pensions, identification cards for family members of a detained-disappeared person, provisions for legal ownership of homes for spouses of the detained-disappeared, guarantees of legitimacy of children born to the wives of the detained-disappeared, and medical, housing, educational and recreational benefits.

The *Agrupación de Familiares de Detenidos y Desaparecidos* (AFDD) also suggested building a monument dedicated to the victims and the construction of a park called "For Life, Truth and Justice" in homage to the detained-disappeared. Such a park was inaugurated on March 24, 1997 at Villa Grimaldi, the site of a concentration camp on the edge of Santiago that detained and tortured over 4500 Chilean citizens. The Chilean government restored the old site to transform the symbol of pain into one of peace and hope for all of Chile, thus naming the park, "El Parque por la Paz"—The Park for Peace. The

AFDD proposed that the victim's biographies be published and the theme of human rights be introduced at all educational levels so as to remember and not repeat the events of the past. They also recommended the establishment of scholarships named after the victims and the inclusion of August 30th in the calendar as an official day of commemoration (the National Day of the Detained-Disappeared).[7]

In accordance with its promise to the human rights organizations, the Aylwin government promulgated a law authorizing the payment of compensation to the relatives of victims of the repression through the National Corporation for Reparation and Reconciliation.[8] The law established a figure of about 140,000 pesos a month, which would benefit about 2,279 people. Speaking for the AFDD, its president Solá Sierra, said the law "is an important step on the road to truth, although nothing can compensate for the suffering, the sorrow ..."[9] All other suggestions regarding educational and medical benefits have also been implemented to a large extent, but the human rights issue continues to be a divisive one. The Right and the military contend that the question of human rights violations is no longer relevant - violations may have occurred in the past and are now history. The Church is slowly moving away from what it now perceives as a political issue and has chosen to focus on pastoral issues, the youth and the problems of juvenile delinquency. Meanwhile, human rights groups are pressing for the repeal of the Amnesty Law of 1978, believing that guilty military officials must be tried in court. While Aylwin has been pushing for judicial investigations of the human rights violations (under the Aylwin Doctrine), some human rights groups feel betrayed and believe that justice will only be served when the guilty are brought to trial and punished.

The debate of reparations has only continued with President Lagos in office, a member of the ideological left but with neoliberal economic views. Although elected by the people, Lagos won with a small victory, and in turn has gained significant pressure from the opposing sides to moderate his policies. Lagos and his administration continue to push for reparations for all citizens detained and tortured in concentration camps, and to those families who lost a member due to such atrocities. However, Lagos not only faces pressure from his political opponents, but likewise much of the public. Chilean society is still greatly polarized by the political parties, regardless of all of them having neoliberal economic policies. Although most Chileans would agree that such atrocities were bad moments in history, many that side with the Center and Right would argue that they were necessary to move Chile in the right direction and that such reparations would only bring back the past. Nevertheless, Lagos and human rights groups will push for the reparations; although, the former will watch the political polls in the rear view mirror. Amongst the human rights issues throughout the international community, one of them is to bring Pinochet and several of his officers to justice. After being detained in Spain and in England, Pinochet now resides back in Chile, "unable" to face charges because of weak health conditions. Regardless of health concerns, there are several groups, namely International Policy Studies and Amnesty International that are working to bring justice to a murderer.

Survival Groups and the State

With the transition to democracy, the predominantly female *sobrevivencia* organizations that existed under the Pinochet government have decreased not only in membership, but also in terms of numbers of organizations existing in the metropolitan areas. Various reasons have been put forward as plausible explanations: the victory of pro-democracy forces in the Plebiscite, the election of the *Concertación*, the hope that the economic and political situation is going to improve under the democratic government, exhaustion of the members after years of severe repression and protest and the withdrawal of the Church's assistance and solidarity. While the Church assisted the *ollas* up to the end of 1990, beginning January 1991 it moved out, choosing to focus only on pastoral work.

Realizing that these organizations were a consequence of the economic marginalization of the popular sectors, the Aylwin government declared that it was committed to consolidating democracy, which would be inclusive of all Chileans. One of the state's goals was to stimulate growth, efficiency and the competitive potential of small enterprises as well as to encourage equal distribution of the fruits of development. The biggest challenge was to develop models that would permit the expertise and knowledge regarding food programs gathered in the *ollas* to be incorporated in state and non-governmental initiatives.[10] Although the *ollas* were linked closely to people's daily lives and provided essential services in the community, it is important to keep in mind that they were solutions to hunger and poverty and therefore, by definition, not meant to be permanent in nature. However, the *ollas* definitely had a positive influence as far as women's personal growth and social and political participation are concerned, so the state and non-governmental agencies working with the *ollas*, such as *NOVIB, Compartiendo la Mesa, Cooperativa de Liberación, PET, TEKHNE* and *PROSAN*, wished to maintain these essential characteristics of popular participation.

The Aylwin government established the *Fondo de Solidaridad e Inversión Social* (FOSIS), linked to the Ministry of Planning and Cooperation (ODEPLAN), to assist the dispossessed sectors of the population. FOSIS finances, facilitates and strengthens the initiative of community organizations. Its priority lies in installing infrastructures that permit grass-roots organizations to become self-sufficient and autonomous. It has two important goals: to support projects of a productive character that would increase the incomes of poor families and to support social initiatives destined to improve the quality of life in poor communities. These projects are presented to FOSIS by communities, women's groups, municipalities, and NGOs. Its approach is integral and it aims towards self-help by functioning in a decentralized manner through *SERPLAC* (*Secretarias Regionales de Planificación y Cooperación*) which receives project proposals from their respective regions.

By providing materials to the *ollas* so that they can then utilize their experience and knowledge for the production and distribution of food in the schools, FOSIS assists women to become economically productive. FOSIS is currently providing financial aid and other resources to some *ollas* to provide milk and cereal to children's centers and elderly people in the community. FOSIS works with JUNAEB and the *ollas* to implement this project. The *ollas* (with a predominantly female membership) attend to children younger than twelve years and adults older than sixty years, providing them with at least 250 calories per day. These *ollas* are catering to at least twenty thousand aged people in the Metropolitan region of Santiago and Region V. FOSIS also works with organizations in communities where there are no *ollas* to provide similar services.[11]

In order to understand the work that FOSIS does with women and the poor it is worth examining one particular project called the *Proyecto ROCAP*, which involved converting the *ollas* into popular *amasanderias* (bakeries). The project is funded jointly by several NGOs such as *Campaña Compartiendo la Mesa, Cooperative de Liberación, Tekhne, Consultora Tecnica* and *PET*. *Cooperativa Liberación* administers the financial resources, *Tekhne* provides technological support, CT serves as technical consultant, PET provides educational support and *Compaña Compartiendo La Mesa* plays the role of

Institutional Coordinator for the *ollas*. The project began in April 1991, counting on financial assistance from *FOSIS* (thirty percent) and *NOVIB* (seventy percent of the total). In this pilot project, *ollas* have been converted into small-scale local bakeries that produce bread, utilizing about one to 1.5 quintals of flour daily (*Proyecto Rocap* 1991, 17). Even after payments have been made, the *ollas* had enough money to render the whole operation financially possible and provide stable employment for about seventy people (five people per *olla*).

The social effects of projects funded by FOSIS are leading to the development and strengthening of popular women's organizations, while they enrich and supplement family diets. They provide stable employment opportunities for women, ingenuous avenues for development and for the creation of small-scale enterprises that result from the projects. Technically, it enriches and transfers local technologies, and assists in the development of local resources and markets. Psychologically, it fortifies avenues for women's participation and provides leadership opportunities.

Internal Division: Indigenous Women and the Women's Movement

Chile is largely homogenous, with most of its population having both Hispanic and native blood; therefore, differences in Chile are generally easy to spot. Chileans also tend to be fairly blunt about differences, nicknaming people things like *flaco* "skinny", *rubia* "blonde", or *Negro* "black". Due to this, there is an idea throughout the culture that there is no such thing as racism, that all differences are out in the open and people deal with them as such. It follows that the same assumption is cast upon differences between the dominant Spanish culture and that of the Mapuche. Since most Chileans have some percentage of both Spanish and of indigenous in their heritage the general assumption is that there is no division between these cultures.

The problem with this assumption is that it is much too generalized. The standard of living for women in the region of Santiago is not much different for Mapuche women than it is for the overall population. On the other hand, the poverty rates for Mapuche women in areas with large Indigenous populations are double that of the overall population (Mesa Mujer Rural, SERNAM 2002, p 20). Generally the situation for Mapuche women is much worse than that of the overall population in Chile. Mapuche women are more likely to experience domestic violence, less likely to receive credit, and are usually given only a very basic education. The assumption that racial differences are not an issue has done a huge disservice to the Women's Movement in Chile.

The lack of recognition of ethnic differences has led to a void in effective services for Mapuche women. The CONADI, who is generally expected to deal with issues regarding indigenous populations, has not been very involved in issues regarding women. In addition, SERNAM has limited involvement with indigenous populations, focusing most of their initiatives on more urban areas and legislation. Thus, the plight of Mapuche women is largely ignored even by those organizations that have the power to help them. To exacerbate these matters, groups that are specifically oriented to help indigenous women are often left with little funding and organization. Due to these issues, it seems clear that like most women's movements, that of Chile is not without its internal division.

Políticas: Women and Political Parties

Since political parties play a critical role in the current democratic system and their relations with women's organizations have been controversial in the past, it is necessary to turn our attention to this relationship again. Some female party militants (*políticas*) have dual loyalties: to the political party and to women's organizations. They have been criticized by radical feminists for participating in parties that model the concentration of power, patriarchal and hierarchical relations, and the exploitation of women (Molina 1989, 126). The *políticas* continue to raise issues of gender equality within the political parties seeking to avoid ghettoization by turning "women's issues" into "party issues." Their efforts in dealing with these traditional bastions of male power have met with some success, but there is much more to be done.

The Pinochet regime introduced the "sistema binomical mayoritario" which intended to transform the traditional three-thirds party system, which Chile traditionally had, to a bi-party system. According to Borzutsky (1998, 102)

> Each district elects two representatives and each party can present two candidates. Voters choose one candidate and the winners are determined by the total vote received per list. The list with the largest number of votes gets one seat and the second seat is elected from the second list that has at least half of the number of votes.

Most Chileans are of the opinion that these electoral laws essentially tilt the political process in favor of the Right and so as Borzutsky summarizes (1998, 103),

> although the Right does not control either the executive or the legislative branch, it has the power to maintain the system as it is and it can obstruct reforms dealing with the electoral laws, structure and power of the Supreme Court, the autonomy of the armed forces, and the power of groups and individuals, such as the appointed senators, who no popular mandate.

In the post-transition period, the tri-polar party system (Right/Center/Left) re-emerged in the form of a Center-Left bloc and a Right bloc.

In Chile, as far as the Left is concerned, the experience of the dictatorship and increasing gender consciousness on the part of party militants has led to some changes. The *Unión de Mujeres Socialistas* (UMS), made up of female militants of the Socialist party, claims that social relations involve domination, of class, gender, ethnicity, and race. In this context, the UMS has adopted feminism as a mode of struggle to transform the sexist system which characterizes women's relations in the family, society and the polity (Molina 1989, 116). The UMS sees its role in making women more visible within the party, challenging it to develop programs catering not only to its traditional social base, but also considering women as a distinct social group.[12] The UMS supports legal reforms that would establish equal marital rights, guarantee pregnant women the right to work, penalize all forms of sexual harassment, create programs for training women in non-traditional activities, and legalize divorce. The Socialist party (PS) has established positive discrimination, a measure requiring that women constitute a minimum of twenty percent of the party's National Directorate. In 1991, 21.1 per cent of executive positions in the PS were held by women (Valdés and Gomariz 1992, 105). Despite this, female party militants who ascribe to feminism still continue to face a series of problems. The most common one is the accusation that they have abandoned the socialist cause, that they engage in sectionalism and their commitments are divided between the feminist agenda and the party.

The PDC (Christian Democratic Party) continues to have a *Departamento Técnico de la Mujer* (Technical Department for Women) and at the level of the *comuna*, there are a large number of women leaders. But at the higher provincial or national levels, the situation changes (Muñoz 1988). The PDC has not adopted positive discrimination for women but it is the party with the highest female following because it combines centrist thought, emphasis on the family, and affiliation with the Catholic Church. It advocates strengthening the nuclear family and the healthy development of its members to secure a democratic regime.

Consequently the PDC female militants propose

> that equality should be a legal reality and discrimination should be ended. On the basis of solidarity it is possible to construct a society which is more personalized and which permits men and women to not only realize their own personal goals but also to develop creativity for the benefit of the community as a whole. (qtd. in Molina 1989b, 95)

PDC female militants have been criticized by other feminists for being more loyal to the party than to the women's agenda and for presenting the "Woman Question" in terms of the family rather than straight women's rights. This is an accusation levied against SERNAM as well which has been established under the Aylwin (PDC) government.

In the PPD (Party for Democracy), the "Technical Commission on Women" is responsible for incorporating women's issues in the party. The party was the first to introduce twenty percent positive discrimination for women, and in the PPD about forty-five percent of the militants are female; of three hundred *Consejales* (Councilors or Board members), twenty-five percent are female. PPD female militants support SERNAM, legalizing divorce, reforming the labor code, and developing female political leaders.[13]

Two parties that arose during the transition, the *Humanistas* (Humanists), and the *Verdes* (Greens), soon combined to form the *Humanista-Verde* (HV) party. The HV party does not have a separate department for women or a policy of positive discrimination. The humanist conception of politics, centered on the personal development of the individual, is similar to some of the principles of feminism (Molina 1989, 107). So, the HV has a significant number of female militants, especially amongst younger Chilean women; 38.5 per cent of the top executive positions in the HV are held by women (Valdés and Gomariz 1992, 105). The HV also nominated a female presidential candidate, Laura Rodriguez, who was later elected to the Chamber of Deputies and played an important role in introducing legislation on divorce. HV proposes sex education, spread of information, educational reform and empowerment through women's organizations. HV militants are of the opinion that legal reforms should work hand in hand with consciousness-raising amongst women. The party suffered a major setback with the untimely death of Laura Rodriguez in August 1992.

The Communist Party (PC) does not have a specific department for women. PC female militants have worked extensively in human rights organizations, unions and popular economic or "survival" groups. They assert that divorce should be permitted and that abortion decisions, as well as the control of sexuality, are the rights of women. They demand that women should receive equal pay and childcare concessions in the labor force and should be encouraged to participate in social and political arenas but without special treatment.

As far as the Right is concerned, the UDI (Independent Democratic Union) defines women's rights in terms of their roles as wives and mothers. The party is opposed to divorce and birth control and emphasizes the moral superiority of women to encourage political participation with a view of making politics more sensitive to family issues, clean and pure. In the *Partido Renovación Nacional* (PRN), themes such as sexuality, birth control and divorce are regarded as "private" matters which should be left to each person's beliefs and values. The defense of the family is of the utmost importance. As Sebastián Piñera Echeñique, Senator from the PRN, stated,

> I do not believe in positive discrimination, neither do I believe that there should be guarantees for women's participation in the directorates of parties, in the Parliament or in any other organization. I think these sorts of measures would lead to new forms of discrimination or of paternalism that would turn against women. (*Participa* 1990, 193)

As far as social and political participation is concerned, the party believes that barriers to women's participation have been shattered and that plenty of women's organizations such as *Cemas*, encourage women's participation. If women do not participate it is due to lack of time or education.

The political parties in Chile pay a great deal of lip-service to the women's agenda and the concept of gender equality, but the number of women elected both within the parties and to the government tell a different story. Some party members blame positive discrimination for "ghettoizing" women and women's issues, and promoting unqualified candidates while adherents defend it vehemently as an instrument for rectifying structural inequalities and giving women leadership opportunities; but the point is largely moot. Despite discussions of equality within the organizational structures of the party and positive discrimination, the number of women holding positions at the decision-making levels has not increased substantially. Neither has this policy translated into increased representation at the national levels. The Aylwin government, which took over in 1990, had 7 female Deputies of a total of 120 (5.8 percent), and 3 female Senators of a total of 47 (6.4 percent) (Hirmas and Gomariz 1990, 22). Women activists were legitimately disappointed with these results.

Women launched a crusade with the slogan *Más Mujeres Al Parliamento* (More Women in Parliament) during the 1993 election. They tried to fight women's invisibility in the political sphere by claiming: *No Hay Democracia Real is la Mujer No Seta!* (Without women there is no real democracy). In the new Frei government, inaugurated in March, 1994, there are still only 9 women deputies, which constitutes 7.5 per cent of the total and again 3 women senators (Frogman and Valdés 1993, 25).

The struggle for improving women's representation in political parties and in the state obviously has a long way to go. However, largely due to the efforts of the *políticas* (female political militants) and the women's movement in general, Chilean women were successful not only in gaining access to the state and p olitical p arties b ut a lso d irecting n ational a ttention t o w omen's i ssues. It was no small achievement to include women's demands in the political platform of the *Concertación,* which eventually formed the new democratic government. The women's movement institutionalized itself, carving out a space for women in a changed political environment that encouraged them to participate in the politics of the newly democratizing nation.

So far we have focused on the political strand of the women's movement and its interaction with the political parties. In the following section we turn to the independent feminists and the cultural dimension of the women's movement.

Feministas: Women and Change in Civil Society

The *feministas* represent a strand of the women's movement working outside of the state and political parties for the formation and growth of a collective i dentity b ased o n g ender. T he *feministas a utónomas* (independent feminists) advocate political bipartisanship and would rather channel their energies into developing gender consciousness, the empowerment of women and subsequent cultural change. An analysis of these organizations is important in order to avoid subjecting the women's movement in Chile to a "political overload."

Consciousness-raising groups are essential for the personal and collective empowerment of women. Discussing the impact of such groups in American feminism, Buckler (1990, 72) writes that consciousness-raising, while "providing daily illustrations of the claim that the personal is the political" creates strong bonds of sisterhood, identifies immediate changes in individual lives and links personal change and societal transformation. Chilean feminists believe that one can and should change one's own life while struggling for social change. Once they have experienced group participation, few women can return to their former way of thinking. Group participation helps build personal and collective consciousness and assists women in identifying problems common to all and then finding solutions.

One of the objectives of feminist thought is the transformation of existing structures (Carrillo 1986). This implies increasing women's participation in existing institutions, as well as the creation of alternative institutions based on feminist thinking and goals. Currently, feminist institutions dedicated to the needs of Chilean women serve not only as concrete manifestations of the women's movement, but also as "female spaces" that nurture common identities and solidarity among women. They provide avenues for leadership and an impetus for self-growth and collective consciousness.

In an article analyzing the feminist movement in the U.S., Mary Fantod Hartenstein declares that

> the form of feminist activism that fuels debates and conversations has changed ... the consciousness-raising functions of street politics ... have been succeeded by a process of what might be termed unobtrusive mobilization inside institutions. (1990, 27)

Similarly, in Chile, what exists now is a "feminist community" that manifests itself in disparate formal organizations, with varying resources and ideological preferences that are localized (primarily in Santiago) and loosely linked. The leaders and professionals of these organizations are all known to each other. They sponsor joint programs, workshops and conferences. These women's groups are characterized by multiple activities, part-time political action, personal involvement and solidarity. This plurality represents a necessary reaction to the changing political conditions but diversity as a goal in itself is also upheld by a large number of Chilean feminists.

The most important legacies of the human rights and feminist strands of the women's movement have been the creation and maintenance of a community of informally linked activists, capable of mobilization around specific issues related to women. "Since the action is focused on cultural codes, the form of the movement is a message, a symbolic challenge to the dominant patterns" (Melucci 1984, 830). While the movement has given birth to a series of formal organizations that may appear dispersed and isolated from each other, a community which cannot be measured could undoubtedly mobilize overtly in a time of crisis. Under President Aylwin, the Commission for Truth and Reconciliation was established to investigate human rights violations that occurred under the dictatorship. The human rights organizations, which are predominantly run by women, have demanded an end to the government's policy of impunity for violators: with the slogan "*No! a la impended!*" However, the democratic government has had limited success since the Amnesty Law of 1978 protects the military against prosecution.

> Sola Sierra, the Chilean human rights leader... argues that "the families [of those who disappeared of were detained and tortured] feel emptiness in the area of moral and public revindication of the victims... that there is a 'veil of impunity' over the human rights abusers and that the Amnesty Law should be either annulled or reformed."

The National Reparation and Reconciliation Commission was created to pay restitution for the families of the victims of human rights abuses. The National Return Office was setup to encourage and simplify the process of reintegration for returning Chilean exiles.

Women who run these centers, funded by NGOs, are professionals who also promote consciousness-raising workshops and undertake research on the situation of women. As Virginia Vargas points out,

> because of the enormous influence they have over other groups of women, principally from the popular sectors, ... they give a certain multi-class character to the movement and function as the nexus between women of the popular and the middle sectors. They serve as a current of transmission of the processes, experiences and practices of the different kinds of women's organizations. (1988a, 12)

These women invariably belong to the parties of the Left (double militants) or are independent feminists, and have developed a highly sophisticated critique of the existing system based on their experiences and understanding of gender discrimination and oppression. Their aspirations are more long-term in orientation since they see built-in limitations in the reform-oriented strategies of the *políticas*. Undoubtedly, they understand that a democratic regime is more amenable to gender issues than an authoritarian one. But their focus on the "feminist" and "autonomous" strand of the women's movement works for the creation and growth of an identity based on gender. Not only do they endeavor to eliminate patriarchal relations, but the existence of their organizations exemplify alternative social arrangements. These organizations are an essential part of the process of preserving the women's movement.

Feminist Organizations and Consciousness-Raising

The expression of radical feminism in Chile is the *Casa de la Mujer La Morada*, which came into existence in October 1983, with the purpose of providing an open space for women meeting to discuss, reflect on and transform their condition of discrimination. *La Morada* institutionalized the *Movimiento Feminista*, which resulted from the realization that subverting women's rights is a fundamental factor in the existence and conservation of all forms of oppression. *La Morada* members pride themselves on being feminist and independent of any kind of state, religious or political entity. They serve as a center of analysis and dissemination of information on the condition of women.[14] They subscribe to individual and collective gender consciousness as a means of fortifying an independent movement and a strategy for liberating women.

Focusing on "formation," *La Morada* members conduct workshops and courses dealing with feminine identity, knowledge of the self, women and politics, and sexuality. They offer free legal aid and have an open house in order to talk about themselves. Wishing to use mass communication to develop gender consciousness, they publish a bi-monthly bulletin and also broadcast a radio program called *Mujeres Hoy* (Women Today) every Saturday morning.

MOMUPO represents a strand of what has been referred to as *feminismo popular* (popular feminism). The organization shares the basic propositions of feminism but emphasizes the problems that affect women of the popular sector in particular. These problems, such as the struggle for survival, class discrimination and *machismo* limit popular women's participation and raise obstacles in the building of a common gender identity.[15] MOMUPO's most distinguishing characteristic is that it is a grass-roots group with base groups of its own. At the same time, its uniqueness lies in its ability to combine class and gender issues to meet the needs of shanty-town women.

MEMCH'83 is a NGO that receives funding from abroad and serves and coordinates social organizations of women.[16] Amongst the most important base groups of this organization are *Acción Femenina* (AF), *Agrupación de Mujeres Democráticas* (AMD), *Unión de Mujeres de Chile* (UCHM), *Comité de Defensa de los Derechos de la Mujer* (CODEM) and *Mujeres de Chile* (MUDECHI). These organizations have publications of their own: *Guacolda, Remolino, Clarita, Vamos Mujer* and *Mudechi* respectively.

The *Instituto de la Mujer* is also a NGO, autonomous and pluralistic in character, that educates and empowers women. It focuses on research in health, work, politics and legislation as they affect women, and it is activist in nature: it denounces acts of discrimination and oppression of women such as domestic violence, rape and sexual abuse in the work place. It also offers professional, legal and psychological services to women and works in the realm of art and culture in order to foster women's integral development.[17]

Some of the women who worked together in the CNMD (Coalition of Women for Democracy) and other independent feminists, created *Mujeres Ahora* (Women Now), an organization whose central aim is to unite and organize women in a democratic and pluralistic manner.[18] It coordinates the activities of NGOs, governmental organizations, centers of research and investigation, and public and private institutions dedicated to women in order to create a unified, centralized women's front. Consequently *Mujeres Ahora* has extremely broad goals such as to influence social decisions with respect to women, to defend women's rights and to denounce discrimination against women. It develops leadership qualities in women to enable them to participate in political parties, local, and national government. *Mujeres Ahora* wants to recognize and empower women, raise consciousness regarding women's rights and build solidarity among women in Chile and abroad.

Other organizations develop and maintain a collective identity and awareness amongst women through the vehicle of service. These organizations receive funds from foreign agencies or international NGOs and provide gender-specific services to common women. They do not have their own grass-roots organizations but they work with other base organizations of women, providing them with various kinds of health, educational and consciousness-raising services. An example of such a non-governmental organization is the *Centro de Servicios y Promoción de la Mujer* (DOMOS), created in 1985 to educate and liberate women by making them mindful of their history and the conditions of their daily lives. It runs a *Programa de Atención Psicológica* which provides psychotherapy services to women. Its *Programa de Educación Preventiva* provides workshops and group experiences regarding women's personal identity, sexuality, menopause, pregnancy, post-partum care and family planning.[19]

RIDEM, or *Red de Información de los Derechos de la Mujer*, is a nongovernmental organization which informs, orients and educates groups of women about their legal, social and economic rights. RIDEM works on the premise that women need information about their rights and the resources which the community is able to offer them. In addition to presenting workshops on women's rights, the organization provides professional and legal assistance as well as psychological and family treatment. RIDEM works with individuals and grass-root organizations of women in five zones of the Metropolitan region.[20]

Another organization similar to RIDEM, called *Tierra Nuestra*, is an *Equipo de Capacitación de la Mujer Pobladora* (Team for the Training of Popular Women). The chief characteristic of this NGO is that it works only with *pobladora* grass-roots organizations called *Talleres de la Mujer Pobladora* that exist in the shantytowns.[21] It contributes to the discovery of the artistic and creative potential of popular women with programs on theater, dance, painting, sewing and ceramics, which reinforce their popular identity and culture. The organization seeks to educate women about their particular situation in society and draws them in the process of democratization. It provides courses on women's legal situations, sexuality, relations between parents and children, and women's rights.

In the outskirts of Santiago, another NGO involved in women's development is *Centro El Canelo de Nos* which encourages the growth of popular technology and alternative forms of communication, and provides legal and professional help for organized groups in the popular sectors. It works on the belief that people possess the essential capabilities to control their own lives at both the personal and the social level. It has a network of centers not only in Chile but also throughout Latin America.

Casas de la Mujer (Houses for Women) are spread throughout the country and, though they are run by different organizations and focus on different issues, their basic service is to provide popular women with a space for meeting and reflection. The programs focus on learning about the rights of women, participating in cultural and recreational activities, sharing experiences, organizing groups for self-help projects, proposing ideas for bettering the situation of women and promoting literacy. Services such as legal aid, psychological and gynecological care, and family planning are provided for free. The upshot of these activities is that the life of the *pobladora* woman is greatly improved. Perhaps the best known of these *casas* is the *Casa Sofia* in Conchalí.

The organizations discussed above combine the simple, everyday "survival" needs of women with "strategic gender interests" through the services and programs they provide. Keeping the socio-economic reality of their clientele in mind, they focus on issues of women's health, reproduction, empowerment and identity and are responsible for the continued existence or "maintenance" of the women's movement. Therefore, women's organizations that provide services of this nature are extremely important; they highlight continuously that the personal is not only public, but political. They also continue to work on establishing democracy in the home and the country, empowering women to fight for their own rights and identity.

Other NGOs research the status of women, sensitizing the population in general and women in particular to the history, the socio-economic reality and cultural conditions that help define Chilean women. Through their research they emphasize the necessity of transforming sexist and hierarchical social relations and structures. CEM, or *Centro de Estudios de la Mujer*, the most important research-oriented NGO, provides information to organizations that work directly with women's groups on training and gender consciousness.[22] *Centro de Desarollo de la Mujer* (CEDEM), another NGO, does research on Mapuche women.

The Unidad de Comunicación Alternativa de la Mujer, part of the Instituto Latinoamericano de Estudios Transnacionales (ILET), is another NGO with a network of publications that provide women with an alternative and gender sensitive means of communication. Its most popular publication, FEMPRESS, consists of articles from the presses of ten Latin American countries, supplemented with articles written by special correspondents analyzing the political, cultural and socio-economic situation of women in their respective countries.

ISIS Internacional serves as a center for information, documentation and communication regarding women. Since 1986, *ISIS* has been computerized, with a data base of bibliographies and abstracts of publications and periodicals. It also has a *Red de Salud de las Mujeres Latinoamericans y del Caribe* and publishes various journals regarding women's health. It runs a *Programa de Información y Políticas sobre Violencia en Contra de la Mujer en América Latina y el Caribe* and publishes information regarding the situations, reforms and institutions that work to prevent violence against women. Its most important publication is *Ediciones de las Mujeres*, a women's book series that is published twice a year in English and Spanish and edited in collaboration with women's groups from the Third World.[23]

The work of these organizations is crucial not only because they make gender-specific research available, but also because they encourage critical thinking and debate regarding the best possible ways to solve the problems of inequality and discrimination that women face. They also disperse information regarding Chilean and other Third World women, both nationally and internationally. Feminist organizations continue struggling to influence the social and historical project of society in a period of the democratic transition. Their struggle is now more creative than defensive since with the establishment of a democratic government society has opened up; social arrangements are not as authoritarian and the ideological-cultural model espoused by the military is being strongly questioned. However, the contest continues for control over the historical project and society's direction along with the debate over the role of women as autonomous agents in building a new Chile.

Campaigns, Conferences and Celebrations

The Chilean women's movement expresses itself openly throughout the world with the celebration of the International Women's Day, first held in 1989 in the Santa Clara stadium. In spite of ideological and social differences, women workers, peasants, professionals, artists and housewives, organized and unorganized, were present. Because the democratic government was in power, the 8th of March 1991 event was different than in the past; a big fair was held in Estación Mapocho, where women exhibited their history with its joys, sorrows, hopes, challenges and struggles.

Campaigns provide another form of drawing attention and mobilizing women around very specific issues. They sensitize people and draw attention to issues usually relegated to the realm of the "private" and not discussed, raising questions that were previously not considered permissible or worthy of concern. A massive campaign on the rights of women was initiated in July 1989; its slogan was *Soy Mujer ... Tengo Derechos* (I am a Woman ... I Have Rights). In November 1990, a campaign against domestic violence and violence against women resulted from the 25th November "International Day of No More Violence Against Women," declared by the 1st Latin American and Caribbean Feminist Conference held in Bogota in 1981. In 1991, a massive campaign for women's health was launched with the slogan "I am a Woman and I Want Health." Since 1991, the Decade for *Educación Humana No Sexista* (Non-Sexist Education) in Latin America, various Chilean women's organizations participated in the campaign *Trabajemos por una Educacion No Sexista* to emphasize discrimination in education. Women's organizations all over the country supported these campaigns, showing they were capable of collaborative effort and united work.

Feminist organizations, whether research, action or service-oriented express the cultural message of the women's movement. They were and are vital because the theme of women and the "Woman Question" occupies primacy in these organizations and in the workshops, programs and campaigns they sponsor. Their top priorities are women, women's empowerment and problems confronting women. They assist women in understanding the roots of their oppression and help build their pride and self-esteem, both individually and as groups. Moreover, the continued existence of these organizations is a goal in itself; precisely because these organizations are indicative of alternative cultural patterns and equal social relations and because they provide women with a unique set of experiences.

The outright mobilization of women during the Pinochet days has given way to state and societal institutionalization. Legislative reform, workshops, seminars, conferences, campaigns and multiple organizations are the concrete manifestations of the women's movement in the state, political parties and civil society. Through these strategies and organizations women seek to highlight the fact that the "personal is political," and that changes in the *vida cotidiana* (daily life) are essential to transforming a male-dominated society.

Notes

1. Information on SERNAM and various programs initiated by it was obtained through personal interviews in Chile with individuals familiar with the agency and its work as well as through pamphlets published monthly by the Public Relations Department of the Ministry called *Informe de Actividades Servicio Nacional de la Mujer*.

2. Servicio Nacional de la Mujer, *Qué es el SERNAM*? (Santiago: SERNAM).

3. Departamento de Prensa, *Informe de Actividades Servicio Nacional de la Mujer*, Jan./March 1991. *Mujer/Fempress*, December, 1993.

4. Under the law Chilean marriages can only be nullified, a process that is expensive and time consuming. Gabriel Valdés, an influential Christian Democrat leader, has even suggested a plebiscite on this divisive issue. A survey conducted by CEP-Adimark found that 73.7 per cent of Chileans are in favor of authorizing divorce in some cases. 80 per cent said they approved of the use of contraceptives and 52.5 per cent approved abortion in certain circumstances. 46 per cent were firmly against it (*Southern Cone Report*, Latin American Regional Reports, 26 December, 1991). It is interesting that the survey appeared just a month after Carlos Oveido, Archbishop of Santiago, published a pastoral letter entitled *Moral, Juventud y Sociedad Permisiva*.

5. For more on this see Lilian Mires, Natacha Molina, and M. E. Valenzuela, *Cambio Social, Transición y Políticas Públicas Hacia la Mujer*. Paper presented at the Seminario Internacional Cambio Social, Transición y Políticas Publicas Hacia la Mujer. Santiago, Sept. 1989. Also see *"State Feminism" and Women's Movements: The Impact of Chile's Servicio Nacional de la Mujer on Women's Activism* by Susan Franceschet, 2003. This paper could possibly be one of the strongest arguments for state institutionalization of women's movements in Latin America by referencing Chile.

6. See PRODEMU, *Nuestra Propuesta* (Santiago: PRODEMU). Information was also obtained from interviews conducted with women working for PRODEMU as well as pamphlets and working papers received from this organization. This information is from a coordinated effort between PRODEMU and SERNAM called *Mesa Mujer Rural* or table for the rural woman. This effort put together a lot of the plight and the actions being taken with regard to rural women.

7. This information of the suggestions given by the *Agrupación de Familiares de Detenidos y Desaparecidos* is from *Condición Esencial para la Reconciliación, Caminando por la Verdad se Abrira paso a la Justicia*, and *Respuesta de la Agrupación de*

Familiares de Detenidos y Desaparecidos a la Comisión Nacional de Verdad y Reconciliación (Santiago: AFDD, Vicaría de la Solidaridad).

[8.] The National Commission for Reparation and Reconciliation was created in January, 1992. It was expected to finish its task in 24 months.

[9.] Quoted from the *Southern Cone Report*, Latin American Regional Report, March 12, 1992.

[10.] The limitations of the *ollas* are documented in *Proyecto Rocap* and other working papers of NGOs working with the *ollas*, such as the *Cooperativa Liberación*. Some of the information about problems facing the ollas and the tensions between them and the NGOs was obtained through interviews conducted with members of different *ollas*, with their leaders and with representatives of the NGOs.

[11.] This information was obtained from interviews with officials from FOSIS and JUNAEB, as well as from various pamphlets issued by FOSIS, describing its goals and activities.

[12.] This information was obtained through interviews with female members of the Socialist party.

[13.] Information obtained through interviews with female members of the PPD.

[14.] All information is taken from interviews with various members of *La Morada* as well as from pamphlets published by the organization, describing its activities, goals and strategies.

[15.] Interview with Coty Silva, a longstanding and influential member of MOMUPO.

[16.] Information obtained from interviews with members and leaders of MEMCH.

[17.] Information on the activities of the *Instituto de la Mujer* was obtained through personal interviews and pamphlets published by the Institute.

[18.] Interview with Josefina Rossetti and Carmen Gloria Aguayo, who are among the founders of *Mujeres Ahora*.

[19.] Interviews with members of DOMOS.

[20.] Information obtained from conversations with professional working for RIDEM, as well as from RIDEM's monthly newsletters.

[21] Interviews with leaders of *Tierra Nuestra*.

[22] Interview with Rosalba Todaro, Director of CEM.

[23] Interview with María Soledad Weinstein, Director of ISIS, and members of the organization.

Conclusion

The introduction established that one of the goals of this book was to analyze the conditions that led to the genesis of an independent women's movement in Chile after 1973. If relative deprivation, Church support and grass-roots organizations were sufficient to explain the rise of the women's movement, then the movement could have arisen a long time before the military government. It is imperative to understand that the military government's policies toward women severely exacerbated the existing situation. Chapter one outlined in detail the military's cultural-ideological model for women. The military government understood the importance of female support, and set out to court and win women over to its side. The authoritarian government pursued a carefully considered policy that emphasized the traditional role of women as mothers, wives and protectors of the fatherland. They sought women out as partners in the building of a new authoritarian Chile; however, this partnership had serious shortcomings which became evident when the military implemented its vision of society and the economy. The military government perceived women as obedient adherents to traditional sexual roles who would preserve the dichotomy of the private and the public. An increasing number of women, however, envisaged a completely different role for themselves, which compelled them to become active opponents of the regime.

The analysis in the second chapter described how the socio-economic conditions, the infrastructure provided by the Church and the Christian Base Communities, along with existing popular organizations, provided the essential structures and space for the rise of an autonomous women's movement. But explanations focusing only on structures and socio-economic policies are not sufficient to explain the rise of the movement. The impetus for its rise was the emergence of an alternative vision of society and the growth of a gender-based collective identity among Chilean women. The explicit articulation of this alternative vision based on a critique of authoritarianism and patriarchy and strong respect for human rights, equality and participation was largely due to the efforts of the feminists. Participation of women prior to 1973 was controlled and manipulated by the governments and ruling elites in favor of their own political interests. Since some women's organizations were also affiliated with the authoritarian government and dominated by the traditional image and role of women, women were among the greatest supporters as well the strongest opponents of the military government. This indicates the existence of two opposing visions and sets of values for women.

Women's organizations that grew in this period advocated relations of equality and independence against military domination. The women's movement was successful in introducing not only new forms of organization, but also new issues of discussion into the political agenda. Human rights groups demanded respect for individual liberties and limitations of state powers. In doing so, they emphasized the rights of all Chileans, and women in particular. Since the state only provided limited social services for the marginalized, it was left to the initiative of the people to feed themselves through "survival" groups, which also questioned the existing authoritarian patriarchal system.

Not only were the agents of social change new, but the content of women's demands were novel as well. They sought to politicize the private and include issues of *vida cotidiana* (daily life) into the realm of politics, so that women could participate in the public and national life. They called for a reconceptualization of the political by linking democracy within the nation to democracy within the home. Equal and democratic relations between family members were essential for the elimination of authoritarianism and militarization within state and society.

The Women's Movement and the Transition to Democracy

In order to understand social movements in periods of democratic transitions and change, it is imperative to comprehend the political processes, negotiations and alliance-building in existence. The Chilean women's movement assisted not only in the transition to democracy, but also in its reconstruction, deepening and extension as well. It did so through intense mobilization and insistence that its demands be included in the national agenda prior to the Plebiscite of 1988, and in the national presidential and parliamentary elections that followed it. By building unified opposition to the military government and campaigning for the victory of the "No" in the Plebiscite, women developed new relations with political parties. Eventually, women realized that they could not be completely removed from the political parties and hope to have mass appeal as well. If it wished to extend its public appeal and be successful in mobilizing women, the movement would have to work with the political parties to achieve gender specific goals to which the party elites were also committed.

While the feminists contended that alliances with political parties and the state would co-opt women's goals, the political militants argued that maintaining autonomy would amount to isolation for the movement and its isolation from mainstream polities. Since complete autonomy would translate to being peripheral to politics and thus having limited appeal, the women's movement cooperated with political parties to include women's demands in the national agenda and to gain enough political power to translate their demands into legislation and government policy.

Since the women's organizations that arose during the dictatorship were predominantly independent of political parties (although some of its members and leaders were political party militants), a model of relations between social organizations and political parties was developed.

The importance of structural and organizational autonomy with a free flow of individuals with commitments to both social movements and political parties proved imperative. Such a model continues to permit the co-existence of political parties and social movements, and is conducive to a fair amount of autonomy for both. Because the women's movement in Chile enjoyed a diversity of organizations and tendencies, it was able to become politically effective without completely losing its autonomy. It was able to cooperate with the state and the political parties and convert itself from a social to a political force precisely because of the ability of the feminists and the political militants to adopt different strategies under a unified front. The uniqueness of the Chilean women's movement lies in its diversity and political effectiveness; it functions as a varied social movement with a powerful political dimension. The existence and strategies of the political militants allows for adding women's issues to political party platforms, such as in the case of the PDC and the PS in Chile, while the diversity and numbers of the majority of members lends the movement social clout.

Thus, the Chilean women's movement was successful in generating ingenious mechanisms of representation in the public sphere. The women's movement continues to exist in a Chile engaged in democratic reconstruction, but its form and expression changes with the needs of the day. Women still continue to advocate a vision of society that entails struggle against patriarchal, unequal relations in a male-dominated society. The movement's vision centers upon establishing true democracy in the country and in the home; however, as Slater (1991, 36) writes, "how resistance and opposition are articulated will depend, in large part, on the balance of political forces and the power of competing discourses." Since the women's movement emerged from independent women's organizations in civil society before it entered mainstream politics, its roots go deep enough that the state has thought it necessary to cooperate with women's organizations as well. The first democratic government established SERNAM to function as a Ministry for Women and the political parties have agreed to a twenty to twenty-five percent positive discrimination for women.

The organizational strength of the women's movement lies in NGOs run and dominated by women. These institutions, run by female professionals, are the purest form of mobilization around "strategic gender" interests. They are in accord with the goals of feminism and exemplify the alternative vision of women as they emphasize internal democracy, rotating leadership and a lack of vertical hierarchies; they also seek to democratize daily life and publicize gender issues. The feminists working within civil society demonstrate that it is just not sufficient to democratize social, economic and political institutions; it is equally important to democratize the daily life of women and the issues that concern them.

Despite its impressive list of achievements, the Chilean women's movement continues to grapple with a number of challenges. The movement must consistently and consciously make an effort to strike a balance between diversity and unity. Related to this is the delicate balance between organization and flexible, adaptable structures. The movement depends a great deal on the existence of institutions and centers dedicated to the growth of gender consciousness through international financing and the solidarity of international feminism. In addition to dealing with problems and shortages of finances, the challenge for the movement lies in the need to encourage the growth of intermediary organizations to link the grass-roots organizations to the foreign NGOs; it is important to develop these mid-range organizations.

Another challenge revolves around elaborating the concept of feminism to address the realities of all women and not just middle-class, professional women. This could he achieved through increased understanding and consciousness of the existing reality, position and experiences of different women from different classes and sections of society. Subordination and oppression should be understood in relation to women's social, economic, cultural, educational and family position. Women need to realize that no one group is more important than another, and that all are part and parcel of the same oppression. Vargas writes that it is important to remember that relations of gender are lived in a specific and particular manner, in accordance with the weight of other subjective positions, and women establish connections in different moments of their lives with multiple subordinations (1 99 I 1 2)

The problems of class and gender should be dealt with simultaneously in order to increase the appeal of the movement, encourage all women to participate and meet the demands of a larger number of women. Feminists in Chile must constantly remember the importance of working class women's support for the women's liberation movement; otherwise, they will make the mistake identified by Epstein (1990) as characteristic of the New Social Movements, that is, a lack of interest in the working class. It is important to keep in mind class, cultural, generational and situational differences and this can be done by making the women's movement less ideological and oriented more towards responding to concrete problems and issues (Vargas 1991). Instead of limiting itself to the realm of theory, it needs to increasingly elaborate on both theory and reality and work to increase the participation of women in politics. Popular sector women especially, with their unique experiences gained through participation in the social movements and civil society, must be encouraged to partake in the decision-making processes. Women's participation in politics is limited not because they are uninterested, but because the issues in the typical political realm concern them only remotely. When the issues discussed are important to women, then their participation increases substantially.

Another challenge revolves around eliminating the false dichotomy between the realm of the public and the private. As Howard argues,

> it is not possible to define the political for all time; what is and what is not political changes with the emergence of new questions, posed by new modes of behavior, or new types of social relations. (qtd. in Slater 1991, 37)

Women are deeply immersed both in the process of production and reproduction; for them, the dichotomy between the private and public is artificial at best.

Since some Chilean women still have the impression that feminism is anti-family and does not represent their needs, defined in terms of marriage, family and children, the movement needs to emphasize women's family and individual rights. This important cultural fact should not be overlooked while determining the goals to be met and strategies to be pursued. Historical experience shows that Chilean women are not necessarily conservative, but that they do prefer non-violent, non-confrontational politics; they value the home and the family and desire stability in everyday life. As Mariana Aylwin writes, this inclination and propensity for slow change rather than radical change, as it affects the family, is a cultural rather than a political characteristic of Chilean women.

According to Adriana Santa Cruz, the biggest challenge for the women's movement is maintaining its autonomy from the state and political parties. At the same time,

> the connections between the social movement and the political parties should be obtained by persons who affiliated to both... we should raise feminist slogans in distinct political spaces; penetrate all political apparatuses (the Church, political parties, the state). (Santa Crux 1986, 90)

As I discussed in the section on the achievements of the women movement in Chile, continuous attempts should be made to maintain this autonomy. The state and political parties have shown themselves to be willing allies of women in the period of the transition, and although to a certain extent there has been a return to politics as usual, women must continue to wedge open this window of opportunity and develop new strategies to meet their goals. SERNAM presented a *Plan de Igualdad de Oportunidades Para Las Mujeres 1994–1999* (Plan for Equal Opportunities for Women 1994–1999) to the Frei administration in 1994, which entailed a comprehensive demand for women's rights in Chile. All women's groups must cooperate in pushing for change in the developmental process.

Building a relation with the state is one of the challenges of the women's movement precisely because no effective model exists. Social movements struggle to maintain their autonomy and yet be political actors and work with political parties and the state. The other pressing need is to analyze the relation of the women's movement to power and how to deal with it. Feminist theory, with its emphasis on equal relations, does not provide models for women and power. A dearth of good female leaders at the national and local level presents another challenge. Most leaders of the movement are now employed by the government and the number of women representatives in decision-making positions is still not very impressive. Not only should the development of leaders at the national, local and regional level be encouraged, but coordination and cooperation should be increased between them.

Coordinating the demands of the movement, the state and the Catholic Church creates another problem. Access to contraception, legalized therapeutic abortion and divorce are the movement's demands to which the Catholic Church is strongly opposed. It will be interesting to follow the resolution of these conflicts in a coalition government that is made up of Christian Democrats and Socialists (who themselves are split on these issues) in a country where the Catholic Church enjoys great power.

Finally whether the balance and unity of action between the feminists and the political militants can be maintained is an interesting question. Equally important is the unity amongst the female political militants of the Center and the Left which will depend to a large extent on the dynamics within the *Concertación* and the relations between the Christian Democrats and the Socialists. There are increasing tensions within the *Concertación* regarding the resolution of human rights issues and the legalization of divorce to name a few. Much of the politics of the growth of democracy and the decomposition of authoritarianism will be determined by the future of the *Concertación*. This in turn will impact and will be influenced by the women's movement.

The Chilean situation continues to be a compelling one where new relations between the women's movement, the state, political parties and civil society are gradually being constructed without any established models to follow. This is what at makes the Chilean women's movement worthy of investigation for academics and activists alike.

Bibliography

Alaminos, Antonio. 1989. Percepción de los Partidos Políticos as Comenzar la Transición. Documento de Trabajo, No. 422. Santiago: FLACSO.

Allan, Pamela, Margarita Fernández, and Roberto Urmeneta. 1991. *Las Organizaciones Economicas Populares de Consumo 1989–1991*. Cartilla de Capacitiación y Difusión, No. 49. Santiago: PET.

Alvarez, Sonia E. 1990. *Engendering Democracy in Brazil: Women's Movements in Transition Politics*. Princeton: Princeton University Press.

Amin, Samir et al. 1990. *Transforming the Revolution: Social Movements and the World-System*. New York: Monthly Review Press.

Anales de la Universidad de Chile. *Las Mujeres Rurales en el Contexto de la Modernizacion Agraria*. Sexta Serie, 5, October 1997.

Angelo, Gloria. 1990. *Nuevos Espacios y Nuevas Prácticas de las Mujeres en una Situación de Crisis: Hacia el Surgimiento y Consolidación de un Movimiento Social de Mujeres. El Caso de Chile*. Santiago: Centro de Análisis y Difusión de la Condición de la Mujer Casa de La Morada, Informe de Investigación.

Arellano, J. P. and R. Cortázar. 1982. "Del Milagro a la Crisis." *Estudios CIEPLAN*, No. 8. Santiago: CIEPLAN.

Arizpe, Lourdes. 1990. Foreward: Democracy for a Small Two-Gender Planet. In *Women and Social Change in Latin America*, ed. Elizabeth Jelin. New Jersey: Zed.

Arriagada, Genaro. 1988. *Pinochet: The Politics of Power*. Boston: Allen and Unwin.

Arteaga, Ana Maria. 1988. "Politización de lo Privado y Subversion del Cotidiano." In *Mundo de la Mujer: Continudad y Cambio*. Santiago: CEM. 565–91.

Arteaga, Ana Maria and Eliana Largo V. 1989. "Los ONG en el Area de la Mujer y la Cooperación al Desarrollo." In *Una Puerta que se Abre: Los Organismos no Gubernamentales en la Cooperación al Desarrollo*, ed. Rodrigo Egaña Baraona. Santiago: Taller de Cooperación al Desarrollo. 392–56.

Astelarra, Judith. 1985. "Democracia y Feminismo." In *La Otra Mitad de Chile*, ed. María Angélica Meza. Santiago: CESOC. 117–38.

Aylwin, Mariana. 1986. "Sofía Correa, and Magdalena Piñera." In *Percepción del Rol Político de la Mujer*. Santiago: Instituto Chileno de Estudios Humanísticos, Documentos.

Baldez, Lisa. *Why Women Protest: Women's Movements in Chile*. Cambridge University Press, New York, 2002.

Baño, Rodrigo A. 1985. *Lo Social y lo Político. Un Dilema Clave del Movimiento Popular*. Santiago: FLACSO.

_____. 1990a. *Elecciónes en Chile, Otra vez lo Mismo o al Reves*. Documento de Trabajo, No. 454. Santiago: FLACSO.

_____. 1990b. *Tendencias Políticas y Resultados Electorales despues de Veinte Años*. Documento de Trabajo, No. 460. Santiago: FLACSO.

Boneparth, Ellen, ed. 1982. *Women, Power and Policy*. New York: Pergamon.

Bookman, Ann and Sandra Morgen, eds. 1988. *Women and the Politics of Empowerment*. Philadelphia: Temple University Press.
Borja, Jordi, Teresa Valdés, Hernán Pozo, and Eduardo Morales, eds. 1987. *Descentralización del Estado: Movimiento Social y Gestión Local*. Santiago: FLACSO.
Bourque, Susan C. 1989. "Gender and the State: Perspectives from Latin America." In *Women, the State and Development*, ed. Sue Ellen M. Charlton, Jana Everett and Kathleen Staudt. Albany: State University of New York Press. 114–29.
Boyle, Catherine M. *Touching the air: The cultural force of women in Chile*. Selected from *'Viva' Women and Popular Protest in Latin America*. Routledge Publishers, London, 1993.
Brunner, José J. 1983. *Notas sobre la Vida Cotidiana II. Agonia y Protesta de la Sociabilidad*. Material de Discusión, No. 50. Santiago: FLACSO.
———. 1986. *Universidad y Sociedad en América Latina*. Santiago: FLACSO.
———. 1987. "América Latina Entre la Cultura Autoritaria y la Cultura Democrática Legados y Desafios." *Revista Paraguaya de Sociología* 70 (Sept./Dec.): 7–15.
Buechler, Steven M. 1990. *Women's Movements in the United States*. New Brunswick: Rutgers University Press.
Bunster-Burotto, Ximena. 1986. "Surviving Beyond Fear: Women and Torture in Latin America." In *Women and Change in Latin America*, ed. June Nash and Helen Safa. Massachusetts: Bergin and Garvey. 297–325.
Cabrera, R. et al. 1975. *Evaluación de 10 Años de Planificación Familiar en Chile*. Santiago.
Calderón, Fernando, ed. 1986. *Los Movimientos Sociales ante la Crisis*. Buenos Aires: CLACSO.
Calderón, Fernando and E. Jelin. 1987. "Clases Sociales y Movimientos Sociales en América Latina. Perspectivas y Realidades." In *Marginalidad, Movimientos Sociales y Democracia*. Proposiciones, No. 14. Santiago: SUR. 169–87.
Calvo, Robert. 1980. "The Church and the Doctrine of National Security." In *Churches and Politics in Latin America*, ed. Daniel H. Levine. Beverley Hills: Sage. 135–54.
Campero, Guillermo. 1986. "Luchas y Movilizaciones Sociales en la Crisis: Se Constituen Movimientos Sociales en Chile?" In *Los Movimientos Sociales ante la Crisis*, ed. Fernando Calderón. Buenos Aires: CLACSO. 289–307.
———. 1987. *Entre la Sobrevivencia y la Acción Política. Las Organizaciónes de Pobladores en Santiago*. Santiago: Estudios ILET.
Campero, Guillermo and R. Cortázar. 1988. "Actores Sociales y Transición a la Democracia en Chile." In *Estudios CIEPLAN*, No. 25. Santiago: CIEPLAN. 115–58.
Campero, Guillermo and José A. Valenzuela. 1984. *El Sindicalismo Chileno en el Régimen Militar Chileno*. Santiago: Serie Estudios ILET.
Carrillo, Roxana. 1986. "Centros de Mujeres, Espacios de Mujeres." In *Movimiento Feminista Balance y Perspectivas: América Latina y el Caribe*. Ediciones de las Mujeres, No. 5. Santiago: Isis Internacional. 34–40.

Cavarozzi, Marcelo and M. A. Garretón, eds. 1989. *Los Partidos Políticos en el Autoritarismo y las Transiciónes del Cono Sur*. Santiago: FLACSO.
Centro de Estudios de la Mujer. 1988. *Mundo de Mujer: Continuidad y Cambio*. Santiago: CEM.
Centro El Canelo de Nos. 1990. *Mujer y Democracia: Algunos Antecedentes y Reflexiones*. Serie Documentos de Estudio Programa Mujer, No. 11. Santiago: Centro El Canelo de Nos.
CESIP, Area Mujeres. 1985. *Reflexiones sobre Movimiento Popular de Mujeres y Feminismo*. Nov. mimeo.
———. 1986. *Las Organizaciones Populares de Mujeres: Transformación y Revalorización del Trabajo Femenino*. Sept. mimeo.
Chafetz, Janet Saltzman and Anthony Gary Dworkin. 1986. *Female Revolt: Women's Movements in World and Historical Perspective*. Totowa, N.J.: Rowman and Allanheld.
Charlton, Sue Ellen M., Jana Everett, and Kathleen Staudt, eds. 1989. *Women, the State and Development*. Albany: State University of New York Press.
Chateau, Jorge et al, ed. 1987. *Espacio y Poder: Los Pobladores*. Santiago: FLACSO.
Chavkin, Samuel. 1985. *Storm over Chile: The Junta under Siege*. Connecticut: Lawrence Hill.
Chuchryk, Patricia. 1984. *Protest, Politics and Personal Life: The Emergence of Feminism in a Military Dictatorship, Chile 1974–1983*. Ph.D. diss. York University.
———. 1989. "Feminist Anti-Authoritarian Politics: The Role of Women's Organizations in the Chilean Transition to Democracy." In *The Women's Movement in Latin America: Feminism and the Transition to Democracy*, ed. Jane S. Jaquette. Boston: Unwin Hyman. 149–84.
———. 1989. "Subversive Mothers: The Women's Opposition to the Military Regime in Chile." In *Women, the State and Development*, ed. Sue Ellen M. Charlton, Jana Everett, and Kathleen Staudt. Albany: State University of New York Press. 130–51.
———. 1994. "From Dictatorship to Democracy: The Women's Movement in Chile." in *The Women's Movement in Latin America: Participation and Democracy*, ed. Jane S. Jaquette. 2nd ed. Boulder: Westview. 65–107.
Cleary, Eda. 1987. *El Papel de las Mujeres en la Política de Chile. Acerca del Proceso de Emancipación de Mujeres Chilenas durante la Dictadura Militar de Pinochet*. Alemania Federal.
Cohen, Jean L. 1983. "Rethinking Social Movements." *Berkeley Journal of Sociology* 28:97–113.
———. 1985. "Strategy or Identity: New Theoretical Paradigms and Contemporary Social Movements." *Social Research* 52(4): 663–716.
Comblin, José. 1979. *The Church and the National Security State*. Maryknoll: Orbis Books.

Coordinación de Organizaciónes Sociales de Mujeres. 1991. *Soy Mujer ... Tengo Derechos*. Santiago: FLACSO-SEPADE.
Cook, Rebecca J. and Dickens, Bernard M. *Human Rights Dynamics of Abortion Law Reform*. Human Rights Quarterly, Johns Hopkins University Press. 25.1 (2003) 1–59.
Costain, Anne N. 1982. "Representing Women: The Transition from Social Movement to Interest Group." In *Women, Power and Policy*, ed. Ellen Boneparth. New York: Pergamon Press. 19–37.
Covarrubias, Paz and R. Franco. 1978. *Chile, Mujer y Sociedad*. Santiago: UNICEF.
Crummett, Maria de los Angeles. 1977. "El Poder Feminino: The Mobilization of Women against Socialism in Chile." *Latin American Perspectives* 4(4): 103–13.
Cusack, David F. 1977. *Revolution and Reaction: The Internal and International Dynamics of Conflict and Confrontation in Chile*. Monograph Series in World Affairs. Vol. 14. Book 3. Denver: University of Denver.
Damián, Gisela Espinosa. 1990. "Feminism and Social Struggle in Mexico." In *Third World/Second Sex*, ed. Miranda Davies. Vol. 2. London: Zed. 31–41.
Davies, Miranda, ed. 1985. *Third World/Second Sex: Women's Struggles and National Liberation*. 3rd Reprint. London: Zed.
_____. 1990. *Third World/Second Sex*. Vol. 2. London: Zed.
De Barbieri, Teresita and Orlandina De Oliveira. 1989. "La Presencia Política de las Mujeres: Nuevos Sujetos Sociales y Nuevas Formas de Hacer Política." In *Caminando Luchas y Estrategias de las Mujeres Tercer Mundo*. Ediciones de las Mujeres, No. 11. Santiago: Isis Internacional. 67–80.
De la Maza, Gonzalo and M. Garcés. 1985. *La Explosión de las Mayorías. Protesta Nacional 1983–1984*. Santiago: ECO.
"Del Amor a la Necesidad." 1991. *El Cielo por Asalto* 2 (Fall): 33–5.
Delsing, Riet, Andrea Rodó, Paulina Saball, and Betty Walker. 1983. *Tipologia de Organizaciónes y Grupos de Mujeres*. Documento de Trabajo, No. 17. Santiago: SUR.
Deere, Carmen Diana and Magdalena León, eds. 1987. *Rural Women and State Policy: Feminist Perspectives on Latin American Agricultural Development*. Boulder: Westview.
Diaz, Gladys. 1985. "Roles and Contradictions of Chilean Women in the Resistance and in Exile." In *Third World/Second Sex: Women's Struggles and National Liberation*, ed. Miranda Davies. 3rd Reprint. London: Zed. 30–9.
Diaz, Ximena B. 1988. "Perfil de Salud de la Mujer en Chile." In *Mundo de la Mujer: Continuidad y Cambio*. Santiago: CEM. 433–81.
Diaz, Ximena and Eugenia Hola. 1988. "La Mujer en el Trabajo Informal Urbano." In *Mundo de la Mujer: Continuidad y Cambio*. Santiago: CEM. 323–75.
Dinges, John. 1983. "The Rise of the Opposition." *NACLA Report* (Sept./Oct.): 15–26.

Dirigentes de Organizaciónes Laborales, de Ollas Comunes y Comprando Juntos. 1989. *Las Organizaciónes de Subsistencia en la Transición a la Democracia.* Serie Trabajo y Democracia 3. Santiago: PET.
Eckstein, Susan, ed. 1989. *Power and Popular Protest. Latin American Social Movements.* Berkeley: University of California Press.
Eder, Klaus. 1985. "The New Social Movements: Moral Crusades, Political Pressure Groups, or Social Movements." *Social Research* 52(4): 869–90.
———. 1982. "A New Social Movement." *Telos* 52 (Summer): 5–20.
Ediciones Feministas. 1988. *Nos/otras.* Santiago.
Educación y Comunicaciónes. 1989. *Los Limites de la Transición y los Desafíos de la Democratización desde la Base.* Taller de Análisis Movimientos Sociales y Coyuntura, No. 5. Santiago: ECO.
———. 1988. *Los Movimientos Sociales frente al Plebiscito.* Taller de Análisis Movimientos Sociales y Coyuntura, No. 2. Santiago: ECO.
Epstein, Barbara. 1990. "Rethinking Social Movement Theory." *Socialist Review* 90(1): 34–65.
Especial-mujer. *Mujer y Democracia.* 2nd ed. Santiago: ILET, Unidad de Comunicacion Alternativa de la Mujer.
Estay, Carlos H. Rubio. 1989. *Haciao la Organización Jurídica de las Organizaciónes Económicas Populares.* Documento, No. 65. Santiago: PET.
Evers, Tilman. 1985. "Identity: The Hidden Side of the New Social Movements in Latin America." In *New Social Movements and the State in Latin America,* ed. David Slater. Amsterdam: CEDLA. 43–71.
Falk, Richard. 1987. "The Global Promise of Social Movements: Explorations at the Edge of Time." *Alternatives* 12(2): 173–96.
"El Feminismo de los '90: Desafíos y Propuestas." 1991. *El Cielo por Asalto* 2 (Fall): 36–40.
Ferguson, Catherine. 1990. "The Poor in Politics: Social Change and Basic Church Communities in Santiago, Lima and Mexico City." Ph.D. diss. University of Denver.
Fisher, Jo. 1993. *Out of the Shadows: Women, Resistance and Politics in South America.* London: Latin America Bureau.
Fleet, Michael. 1985. *The Rise and Fall of Chilean Christian Democracy.* New Jersey: Princeton University Press.
Flisfisch, Angel. 1990. *El Involucramiento Subjetivo de la Mujer en Política: Exploración de Algunas Hipótesis.* Documento de Trabajo, No. 457. Santiago: FLACSO.
Foss, D. A., and R. Larkin. 1986. *Beyond Revolution: A New Theory of Social Movements.* Mass.: Bergin and Garvey.
Foxley, Alejandro. 1982. "Cinco Lecciónes de la Crisis Actual." *Estudios CIEPLAN,* No. 8. Santiago: CIEPLAN.

———. 1986. "The Neoconservative Economic Experiment in Chile." In *Military Rule in Chile. Dictatorship and Oppositions*, ed. J. Samuel Valenzuela and Arturo Valenzuela. Baltimore: Johns Hopkins Press. 13–50.

———. 1987. "Comentario." In *Marginalidad, Movimientos Sociales y Democracia*. Proposiciones, No. 14. Santiago: SUR. 162–3.

Franceschet, Susan. *"State Feminism" and Women's Movements: The Impact of Chile's Servicio Nacional de la Mujer on Women's Activism*. Latin American Research Review University of Texas Press 38.1 (2003) 9–40.

Freeman, Jo. 1982. "Women and Public Policy: An Overview." In *Women, Power and Policy*, ed. Ellen Boneparth. New York: Pergamon. 47–67.

Frohman, Alicia and Teresa Valdés. 1993. *Democracy in the Country and in the Home. The Women's Movement in Chile*. Documento de Trabajo, Serie Estudios Sociales, No. 55. Santiago: FLACSO.

Fruhling, Hugo. 1984. "Repressive Policies and Legal Dissent in Authoritarian Regimes: Chile 1973–1981." *International Journal of the Sociology of Law* 12:351-74.

Fuentes, Marta and Andre Gunder Frank. 1989. "Ten Theses on Social Movements." *World Development* 17(2): 179–91.

Fundació Rafael Campalans. 1988. *La Transición Democrática en Chile*. Barcelona: Fundació Rafael Campalans.

Gallardo, Bernada. 1987. "El Redescubrimiento del Carácter Social del Hambre: Las Ollas Comunes." In *Espacio y Poder: Los Pobladores*, ed. Jorge Chateau et al. Santiago: FLACSO. 171–201.

———. 1989. *La Opiñión de las Mujeres* (Un Ejercicio de Análisis de Encuesta). Documento de Trabajo, No. 426. Santiago: FLACSO.

Galvez, Thelma and Rosalba Todaro. 1988. "La Segregación Sexual en la Industria." In *Mundo de la Mujer: Continuidad y Cambio*. Santiago: CEM.

Galvez, T. Sanchez, F. *Prospectiva Mujer*. Santiago de Chile MIDEPLAN. 1998.

Garretón, Manuel A. 1987. "Las Complejidades de la Transición Invisible. Movilizaciones Populares y Régimen Militar en Chile." In *Marginalidad, Movimientos Sociales y Democracia*. Proposiciones, No. 14. Santiago: SUR. 109–29.

———. 1989a. *The Chilean Political Process*. Trans. Sharon Kellum. Boston: Unwin Hyman.

———. 1989b. *La Posibilidad Democrática en Chile*. Santiago: FLACSO, Cuadernos de Difusión.

———. 1990a. *Las Condiciónes Socio-Politicos de la Inauguración Democratica en Chile*. Documento de Trabajo, No. 444. Santiago: FLACSO.

———. 1990b. *Espacio Público, Mundo Político y Participación de la Mujer en Chile*. Documento de Trabajo, Estudios Sociales, No. 2. Santiago: FLACSO.

———. 1990c. "Partidos Políticos, Transición y Consolidación Democratica." In *Chile, Sociedad y Transición*. Proposiciones, No. 18. Santiago: SUR. 72–84.

_____. 1990d. *Partidos, Transición y Democracia en Chile*. Documento de Trabajo, No. 443. Santiago: FLACSO.
_____. 1991a. *Cultura Politica y Sociedad* 6.
_____. 1991b. *Cultura Política y Sociedad en la Construcción Democrática*. Estudios Sociales, No 6. Santiago: FLASCO.
_____. 1991c. *La Democratización Política en América Latina y la Crisis de Paradigmas*. Estudios Sociales, No. 5. Santiago: FLACSO.
_____. 1991d. *La Transición Chilena. Una Evaluacion Provisoria*. Estudios Políticos, No. 8. Santiago: FLACSO.
Garretón, Manuel A., ed. 1989. *Propuestas Políticas y Demandas Sociales*. Vol. 3. Santiago: FLACSO.
Gaviola, Edda, Lorella Lopresti, and Claudia Rojas. 1986. *Queremos Votar en las Próximas Elecciones. Historia del Movimiento Femenino Chileno 1913–1952*. Santiago: Coedición Centro de Análisis y Discusión de la Condición de la Mujer y Otros.
Gilfeather, Katherine Anne. 1980. "Women Religious, the Poor, and the Institutional Church in Chile." In *Churches and Politics in Latin America*, ed. Daniel H. Levine. Beverly Hills: Sage Publications. 198–224.
Giovanna, Merola. 1985. "Feminismo: Un Movimiento Social." *Nueva Sociedad* 78 (July/August): 112–17.
Goni, German Bravo. 1991. *Los Derechos Humanos como Cultura Política en las Sociedades Contemporáneas*. Documento de Trabajo, Estudios Políticos, No. 9. Santiago: FLACSO.
Habermas, Jurgen. 1981. "New Social Movements." *Telos* 49 (Fall): 33–7.
Hardy, Clarisa. 1985. *Estrategias Organizadas de Subsistencia: Los Sectores Populares frente a sus Necesidades en Chile*. Documento de Trabajo, No. 41. Santiago: PET.
_____. 1986. *Hambre + Dignidad = Ollas Comunes*. Santiago: PET.
_____. 1988. *Organizarse para Vivir. Pobreza Urbana y Organización Popular*. Santiago: PET.
_____. 1989. *La Ciudad Escindida*. Santiago: PET.
Hardy, Clarisa and L. Razeto. 1984. *Los Nuevos Actores y Practicas Populares: Desafios a la Concertación*. Materiales para Discusión, No. 47. Santiago: CED.
Hines, Donetta. 'Mujer' y Chile:en Transición/ Woman and Chile: in Transition. Cornell University. Prepared for Delivery at the 2001 meeting of Latin American Studies Association, Washington DC, September 6–8, 2001.
Hirmas, María Eugenia and Enrique Gomariz. 1990. *La Situación de la Mujer Chilena, en Cifras*. Santiago: SERNAM.
Hola, Eugenia. 1988. "Mujer, Dominación y Crisis." In *Mundo de la Mujer: Continuidad y Cambio*. Santiago: CEM. 13–49.
Huneeus, Carlos. 1987. *Los Chilenos y la Política. Cambio y Continuidad en el Autoritarismo*. Santiago: Instituto Chileno de Estudios Humanisticos.

ILET-CLACSO. 1986. *Los Movimientos Sociales en Chile y la Lucha Democrática.* Santiago: ILET-CLACSO.
Interview: Maria Theresa Alvarez: Director of Female Temporal Workers Campaign, SERNAM. Conducted May 15, 2003.
Interview: Pilar Fica: Coordinator of Prodemu- Cañete. Conducted May7, 2003.
Isis Internacional. 1986. *Movimiento Feminista Balance y Perspectivas: América Latina y el Caribe.* Ediciones de las Mujeres, No. 5. Santiago: Isis Internacional.
_____. 1986. *Mujeres, Crisis y Movimiento: América Latina y el Caribe.* Ediciones de las Mujeres, No. 9. Santiago: Isis Internacional.
_____. 1989. *Caminanado Luchas y Estrategias de las Mujeres Tercer Mundo.* Ediciones de las Mujeres, No. 11. Santiago: Isis Internacional.
_____. 1991. *Transiciónes Mujeres en los Procesos Democráticos.* Ediciones de las Mujeres, No. 13. 2nd ed. Santiago: Isis Internacional.
Jansana, Loreto. 1989. *El Pan Nuestro. Las Organizaciónes Populares para el Consumo.* Santiago: PET.
Jaquette, Jane S., ed. 1989. *The Women's Movement in Latin America: Feminism and the Transition to Democracy.* Boston: Unwin Hyman.
_____. 1994. *The Women's Movement in Latin America: Participation and Democracy.* 2nd ed. Boulder: Westview.
Jelin, Elizabeth. 1987. "El Itinerario de la Democratización. Movimientos Sociales y la Participación Popular." In *Marginalidad, Movimientos Sociales y Democracia.* Proposiciones, No. 14. Santiago: SUR. 146–61.
Jelin, Elizabeth, ed. 1990. *Women and Social Change in Latin America.* New Jersey: Zed.
Jilberto, A. E. Fernández. 1991. "Social Democracy in Latin America: Rethinking Political Movements in Chile." *International Journal of Political Economy* 21(1): 66–90.
Katzenstein, Mary Fainsod. 1990. "Feminism with American Institutions: Unobtrusive Mobilization in the 1980s." *Signs* 1 (Fall): 27–54.
Katzenstein, Mary Fainsod and Carol McClurg Mueller. 1987. *The Women's Movements of the United States and Western Europe.* Philadelphia: Temple University Press.
Keller, Marcela Cabezas. 1991. *Cambio en la Estructura de Consumo Alimenticio en Chile 1969–1988.* Documento de Trabajo, No. 82. Santiago: PET.
Kirkwood, Julieta. 1982. *Ser Politica en Chile: Las Feministas y los Partidos.* Documento de Trabajo, No. 143. Santiago: FLACSO.
_____. 1983. *El Feminismo Como Negación del Autoritarismo.* Santiago: FLACSO.
_____. 1984. *Los Nudos de la Sabiduría Feminista.* Material de Discusión, No. 64. Santiago: FLACSO.
_____. 1985. "Feminismo y Participacion Política en Chile." In *La Otra Mitad de Chile*, ed. María Angélica Meza. Santiago: CESOC. 13–42.
_____. 1985. "Feministas y Políticas." *Nueva Sociedad* 78 (July/Aug.): 62–70.

Klubock, Thomas Millar. *Writing the History of Women and Gender in Twentieth Century Chile.* Hispanic American Historical Review, Duke University Press. 81.3–4 (2001) 493–518.
Kusnetsoff, Fernando. 1985. "Urban and Housing Policies under Chile's Military Dictatorship 1973–1985." *Latin American Perspectives* 14(2): 157–86.
Laclau, Ernesto. 1985. "New Social Movements and the Plurality of the Social." In *New Social Movements and the State in Latin America*, ed. David Slater. Amsterdam: CEDLA. 27–42.
Larraín, Cristina. 1982. *Catastro de Organizaciónes Femeninas de Gobierno.* Santiago: Instituto Chileno de Estudios Humanisticos.
Latin American Bureau. 1983. *Chile, the Pinochet Decade: The Rise and Fall of the Chicago Boys.* London: Latin American Bureau Press.
Lechner, Norbert. 1980. *Vida Cotidiana y Ámbito Público.* Proyecto de Investigación, Documento de Trabajo, No. 103. Santiago: FLACSO.
Lechner, Norbert and Susana Levy. 1984. *Notas sobre le Vida Cotidiana III: El Disciplinamiento de la Mujer.* Material de Discusión, No. 57. Santiago: FLACSO.
Lechner, Norbert, ed. 1982. *Que Significa Hacer Política?* Lima: DESCO.
Leiva Fernando I. and James Petras. 1986. "Chile's Poor in the Struggle for Democracy." *Latin American Perspectives* 51(4): 5–25.
Levine, Daniel H., ed. 1980. *Churches and Politics in Latin America.* Beverly Hills: Sage.
_____. 1986. *Religion and Political Conflict in Latin America.* Chapel Hill: University of North Carolina Press.
Lobo, Elisabeth Souza. 1989. "Las Mujeres en los Espacios Públicos. Los Movimientos Populares en la Sociedad Brasileña Contemporánea." In *Caminande Luchas y Estrategias de las Mujeres Tercer Mundo.* Ediciones de las Mujeres, No. 11. Santiago: Isis Internacional. 59–65.
Maier, Charles S., ed. 1987. *Changing Boundaries of the Political.* Cambridge: Cambridge University Press.
Malic, Danisa and Elena Serrano. 1988. "La Mujer Chilena ante la Ley." In *Mundo de la Mujer: Continudad y Cambio.* Santiago: CEM. 53–93.
Matterlart, Michelle. 1976. "Chile: The Feminine Side of the Coup d'Etat." in *Sex and Class in Latin America*, ed. June Nash and Helen Safa. New York: Praeger.
McAdam, Doug. 1982. *Political Process and the Development of Black Insurgency 1930–1970.* Chicago: University of Chicago Press.
McCamant, John F. 1989. *Domination, State Power and Political Repression.* Denver: mimeo.
Medhurst, Kenneth. 1972. *Allende's Chile.* New York: St. Martin's.
Melucci, Alberto. 1980. "The New Social Movements: A Theoretical Approach." In *Social Science Information*, 19(2). Beverly Hills: Sage. 199–226.

_____. 1984. "An End to Social Movements? Introductory Paper to the Session on New Movements and Change in Organizational Forms." In *Social Science Information*, 23(4/5). Beverly Hills: Sage. 819–35.

_____. 1985. "The Symbolic Challenge of Contemporary Movements." In *Social Research* 52(4): 789–816.

_____. 1988. "Social Movements and the Democratization of Everyday Life." In *Civil Society and the State*, ed. John Keane. London: Verso. 245–60.

Memoria CEMA-Chile. 1981.

Memoria 1973–83.

Mesa de Mujeres Rural: Una Experiencia de Participación, SERNAM 2002.

Mérola, Giovanna. 1985. "Feminismo: Un Movimiento Social." *Nueva Sociedad* 78 (July/August) 112–7.

Meza, María Angélica, ed. 1985. *La Otra Mitad de Chile*. Santiago: Instituto para el Nuevo Chile.

Mires, Lilian, Natacha Molina, and Marìa Elena Valenzuela. 1989. *Cambio Social, Transición y Políticas Publicas Hacia la Mujer*. Paper presented at the Seminario Internacional Cambio Social, Transición y Políticas Publicas hacia la Mujer. Santiago, September.

Molina, Natacha. 1989a. *Lo Femenino y lo Democratico en el Chile de Hoy*. Santiago: Vector Documents.

_____. 1989b. "Propuestas Políticas y Orientaciónes de Cambio en la Situación de la Mujer." In *Propuestas Políticas y Demandas Sociales*, ed. Manuel Antonio Garreton. Vol. 3. Santiago: FLACSO. 31–171.

_____. 1991. "El Estado y las Mujeres: Una Relación Dificil." In *Transiciónes: Mujeres en los Procesos Democráticos*. Ediciones de las Mujeres, No. 13. 2nd ed. Santiago: ISIS Internacional. 85–97.

Molina, Natacha and C. Serrano. 1988. *Las Mujeres Chilenas Frente a la Política*. Santiago: Instituto de la Mujer.

Molyneux, Maxine. 1986. "Mobilization without Emancipation? Women's Interests, State and Revolution." In *Transition and Development: Problems of Third World Socialism*, ed. Richard R. Fagen, Carmen Diana Deere and José Luis Coraggio. New York: Monthly Review Press. 280–302.

Montecino, Sonia and Josefina Rossetti, eds. 1990. *Tramas para un Nuevo Destino. Propuestas de la Concertación de Mujeres por la Democracia*. Santiago.

Moya-Raggio, Eliana and Ximena Zuñiga. 1988. "Women's Survival and Resistance Strategies: Examples from Chile, 1973–1988." *Michigan Feminist Studies* 4 (Fall): 13–35.

Mujer/fempress. *Demandas de las Mujeres*. Especial. Santiago: ILET, Unidad de Comunicación Alternativa de la Mujer.

_____. *Tensiones entre Machismo y Feminismo*. Santiago: ILET, Unidad de Comunicación Alternativa de la Mujer.

Munizaga, Giselle and Lilian Letelier. 1988. "Mujer y Régimen Militar." In *Mundo de la Mujer: Continuidad y Cambio*. Santiago: CEM. 525–62.

Muñoz, Carolina. 1988. "En los Partidos Políticos También Invisibles?" In *Nos/otras*. Santiago.
Muñoz Dalbora, Adriana. 1987. *Fuerza Feminista y Democracia. Utopía a Realizar*. Santiago: Vector Documents.
Muñoz, Oscar, ed. 1990. *Transición a la Democracia. Marco Político y Económico*. Santiago: CIEPLAN.
Nash, June and Helen Safa, eds. 1976. *Sex and Class in Latin America*. New York: Praeger.
———. 1986. *Women and Change in Latin America*. South Hadley, Ma.: Bergin and Garvey.
Neuse, Steven M. 1978. "Voting in Chile: The Feminine Response." In *Political Participation in Latin America*, ed. John Booth and Mitchell Seligson. New York: Holmes and Meier. 129–44.
O'Donnell, Guillermo A., Philippe C. Schmitter, and Laurence Whitehead, eds. 1986. *Transitions from Authoritarian Rule: Prospects for Democracy*. Baltimore: Johns Hopkins University Press.
Offe, Claus. 1987. "Challenging the Boundaries of Institutional Politics: Social Movements Since the 1960s." In *Changing the Boundaries of the Political*, ed. Charles S. Maier. Cambridge: Cambridge University Press. 63–105.
Oppenheim, Lois. 1985. "Democracy and Social Transformation: The Debate within the Left." *Latin American Perspectives* 46(3): 59–76.
Oxhorn, Philip. 1986. *Democracia y Participación Popular: Organizaciónes Poblacionales en la Futura Democracia Chilena*. Santiago: FLACSO, No. 44.
———. 1991. "The Popular Sector Response to an Authoritarian Regime: Shantytown Organizations Since the Military Coup." *Latin American Perspectives* 18(1): 66–91.
Paramio, Ludolfo. 1985. "Lo Que Todo Marxista Vulgar Debe Saber sobre Feminismo." *Nueva Sociedad* 78 (July/August): 80–8.
Paris Latin American Women's Group. 1985. "Why an Autonomous Women's Movement?" In *Third World/Second Sex: Women's Struggles and National Liberation*, ed. Miranda Davies. 3rd Reprint. London: Zed. 175–9.
Participa. 1990. *Existe la Vocación Política de la Mujer?* Santiago: Participa.
Plan de Igualidad entre Mujeres y Hombres: 2000–2010. SERNAM.
Pozo, Hernán. 1986. *La Participación en la Gestión Local para el Gobierno Autoritario*. Documento de Trabajo, No. 287. Santiago: FLACSO.
———. 1987. "La Participacion en la Gestión Local para el Régimen Actual Chileno." In *Descentralización del Estado: Movimiento Social y Gestión Local*, ed. Jordi Borja, Teresa Valdès, Hernán Pozo, and Eduardo Morales. Santiago: FLACSO. 321–48.
———. 1990. *La Reforma del Régimen Municipal Propuesta por el Gobierno*. Estudios Sociales, No. 3. Santiago: FLACSO.

Proyecto Rocap. 1991. *Reconversión de las Ollas Comunes en Amasenderías Populares*. Santiago: Proyecto Rocap.
Raczynski, Dagmar and Claudia Serrano. 1984. "La Cesantia: Impacto Sobre las Mujer y Familia Popular." In *Estudios CIEPLAN*, No. 14. Santiago: CIEPLAN. 61–97.
_____. 1986. *Vivir la pobreza. Testimonios de Mujeres*. 2nd ed. Santiago: CIEPLAN.
Ramirez, Apolonia. 1986. *Comprando Juntos Frente al Hambre*. Santiago: PET.
_____. 1988. *Renacer en Conchali. Sindicato de Trabajadores Independientes*. Santiago: PET.
Rammsy, Claudio and Raúl Rosales. 1990. "Iglesia y Transición: Notas para un Marco Interpretativo." In *Chile, Sociedad y Transición*. Proposiciones, No. 18. Santiago: SUR. 192–200.
Razeto, Luis M. 1990. *Economía Popular de Solidaridad: Identidad y Proyecto en Una Visión Integradora*. Santiago: PET.
Razeto, Luis M., Arno Klenner, Apolonia Ramirez, and Roberto Urmeneta. 1990. *Las Organizaciónes Económica Populares 1973–1990*. 3rd ed. Santiago: PET.
Rosenberg, Martha I. 1991. "Diferencias y Desigualdades: Acerca del V Encuentro Feminista Latinoamericano y del Caribe." *El Cielo por Asalto* 2 (Fall): 25–31.
Rosenberg, Rina. 1982. "Representing Women at the State and Local Levels: Commissions on the Status of Women." In *Women, Power and Policy*, ed. Ellen Boneparth. New York: Pergamon. 38–46.
Rossetti, Josefina. 1988. "La Educación de las Mujeres en Chile Contemporaneo." In *Mundo de Mujer: Continuidad y Cambio*. Santiago: CEM. 97–181.
Rossetti, Josefina, ed. 1991. *Ideas para la Acción: Encuentro de la Concertación de Mujeres por la Democracia*. Santiago.
Saa, María Antonieta. 1988. "La Lucha Democrática de las Mujeres." In *La Transición Democrática en Chile*, ed. Fundació Rafael Campalans. Barcelona: Fundació Rafael Campalans. 109–18.
Safa, Helen Icken. 1990. "Women's Social Movements in Latin America." *Gender and Society* 4(3): 354–69.
Santa Cruz, Adriana. 1986. "Feminismo Latinoamericano: Los Retos Frente al Poder. Conversación con Adriana Santa Cruz." In *Movimiento Feminista Balance y Perspectivas América Latina y el Caribe*. Ediciones de las Mujeres, No. 5. Santiago: Isis Internacional. 89–94.
Schkolnik, Mariana and Berta Teitelboim. *Pobreza y Desempleo en Poblaciones. La Otra Cara del Modelo Neoliberal*. Colección Temas Sociales 2. Santiago: PET.
Schneider, Cathy. 1991. "Mobilization at the Grassroots: Shantytowns and Resistance in Authoritarian Chile." *Latin American Perspectives* 18(1): 92–112.
Scott, Alan. 1990. *Ideology and the New Social Movements*. London: Unwin Hyman.
SERNAM. 1994. *Plan de Igualdad de Oportunidades para las Mujeres 1994–1999*. Santiago: SERNAM.

Serrano, Claudia. 1985. "Chile, Mujeres en Movimiento." *La Otra Mitad de Chile*, ed. María Angélica Meza. Santiago: CESOC. 73–80.

———. 1988. "Pobladoras en Santiago: Algo Más Que la Crisis." In *Mujeres, Crisis y Movimiento: América Latina y el Caribe*. Ediciones de las Mujeres, No. 9. Santiago: Isis Internacional. 73–80.

———. 1991. "Entre la Autonomía y la Integración." *Transiciones: Mujeres en los Procesos Democráticos*. 2nd ed. Ediciones de las Mujeres, No. 13. Santiago: ISIS Internacional. 99–105.

Silva, María de la Luz. 1986. *La Participación Política de la Mujer en Chile. Las Organizaciónes de Mujeres*. Buenos Aires: Fundación Friedrich Neumann.

Slater, David. 1991. "New Social Movements and Old Political Questions: Rethinking State-Society Relations in Latin American Development." *International Journal of Political Economy* 21(1): 32–65.

Smith, Brian H. 1980. "Churches and Human Rights in Latin America: Recent Trends on the Subcontinent." In *Churches and Politics in Latin America*, ed. Daniel H. Levine. Beverly Hills: Sage. 155–93.

———. 1982. *The Church and Politics in Chile: Challenges to Modern Catholicism*. Princeton: Princeton University Press.

———. 1986. "Chile: Deepening the Allegiance of Working-Class Sectors to the Church in the 1970s." In *Religion and Political Conflict in Latin America*, ed. Daniel H. Levine. Chapel Hill: University of North Carolina Press. 156–86.

Soto, Laura. 1985. "La Mujer, Ciudadana de Segunda Clase?" In *La Otra Mitad de Chile*, ed. María Angélica Meza. Santiago: CESOC. 139–147.

Staudt, Kathleen A. 1982. "Bureaucratic Resistance to Women's Programs: The Case of Women in Development." In *Women, Power and Policy*, ed. Ellen Boneparth. New York: Pergamon. 263–81.

Stepan, Alfred, ed. 1989. *Democratizing Brazil: Problems of Transition and Consolidation*. New York: Oxford University Press.

Stevens, Evelyn P. 1976. "Marianismo: The Other Face of Machismo in Latin America." In *Female and Male in Latin America*, ed. Ann Pescatello. Pittsburgh: Pittsburgh University Press. 89–101.

Timerman, Jacobo. 1987. *Chile: Death in the South*. New York: Knopf.

Tinsman, Heidi. *Good Wives and Unfaithful Men: Gender Negotiations and Sexual Conflicts in the Chilean Agrarian Reform, 1964–1973*. Hispanic American Historical Review, Duke University Press. 81.3–4 (2001) 587–619.

Touraine, Alain. 1981. *The Voice and the Eye: An Analysis of Social Movements*. Trans. Alan Duff. New York: Cambridge University Press.

———. 1983. *Solidarity: The Analysis of a Social Movement*. Trans. David Denby. New York: Cambridge University Press.

———. 1985. "An Introduction to the Study of Social Movements." *Social Research* 52(4): 749–87.

———. 1987. *Actores Sociales y Sistemas Políticos en América Latina*. Santiago: PREALC.

_____. 1988. *Return of the Actor: Social Theory in Postindustrial Society*. Minneapolis: University of Minnesota Press.
Urmeneta, Roberto. 1990. *Las Organizaciónes Económicas Populares. Resultados del Catastro 1989*. Cartilla de Capacitación y Difusión, No. 42. Santiago: PET.
Valdés, Teresa. 1987a. "El Movimiento de Pobladores: 1973–1985. La Recomposición de las Solidaridades Sociales." In *Descentralización del Estado: Movimiento Social y Gestión Local*, ed. Jordi Borja, Teresa Valdés, Hernán Pozo, and Eduardo Morales. Santiago: FLACSO. 263–319.
_____. 1987b. "Ser Mujer en Sectores Populares Urbanos." In *Espacio y Poder: Los Pobladores*, ed. Jorge Chateau et al. Santiago: FLACSO. 203–58.
_____. 1988a. *Mujer, Acción y Debate II. Se Hace Camino al Andar*. Material de Discusión, No. 111. Santiago: FLACSO.
_____. 1988b. *Venid, Benditas de mi Padre. Las Pobladoras, Sus Rutinas y Sus Suenos*. Santiago: FLACSO.
_____. 1991. *Mujer y Derechos Humanos: Menos tu Vientre*. Estudios Sociales, No. 8. Santiago: FLACSO.
Valdés, Teresa and Enrique Gomariz. 1992. *Mujeres Latinoamericanas en Cifras: Chile*. Santiago: Instituto de la Mujer, Ministerio de Asuntos Sociales de España y FLACSO.
Valdés, Teresa and Marisa C. Weinstein. 1989. *Organizaciónes de Pobladoras y Construcción Democrática en Chile*. Documento de Trabajo, No. 434. Santiago: FLACSO.
Valdés, Teresa, M. Weinstein, and A. Malinarich. 1988. *Las Coordinadoras de Organizaciónes Populares. Cinco Experiencias*. Documento de Trabajo, No. 382. Santiago: FLACSO.
Valdés, Teresa, Marisa Weinstein, María Isabel Toledo and Lilian Letelier. 1989. *Centros de Madres 1973–1989: Sólo Disciplinamiento?* Documento de Trabajo, No. 416. Santiago: FLACSO.
Valenzuela, María Elena. 1987. *La Mujer en el Chile Militar: Todas Ibamos a ser Reinas*. Santiago: Ediciones Chile y América, CESOC-ACHIP.
_____. 1990a. "Gender Issues in Chilean Politics." *Peace Review* 4 (Fall): 24–7.
_____. 1990b. "Mujeres y Política: Logros y Tensiónes en el Proceso de Redemocratización." In *Chile, Sociedad y Transición*. Proposiciones, No. 18. Santiago: SUR. 210–32.
_____. 1991. "The Evolving Roles of Women under Military Rule." In *The Struggle for Democracy in Chile 1982–90*, ed. Paul Drake and Ivan Jaksic. Nebraska: Nebraska University Press. 256–97.
_____. 1993. "Las Mujeres y el Poder. Avances y Retrocesos a Tres Años de Democracia en Chile." In *Proposiciones*, No. 22. Santiago: SUR. 249–56.
Valenzuela, Samuel J. and Arturo Valenzuela, eds. 1976. *Chile: Politics and Society*. New Jersey: Transaction Books.
_____. *Military Rule in Chile*. 1986. Baltimore: John Hopkins University Press.
Varas, Agosto. 1980. *Chile, Democracia, Fuerzas Armadas*. Santiago: FLACSO.

Varas, Agosto and F. Aguero. 1978. *Acumulación Financiera, Gobiernos Militares y Seguridad Nacional en América Latina.* Santiago: FLACSO.
Vargas, Virginia. *Movimiento Feminista en el Peru: Balance y Perspectivas.* Lima: Centro de la Mujer Peruana Flora Tristan, mimeo.
———. 1988a. *El Aporte de la Rebeldía de las Mujeres.* Dominican Republic: CIDAF.
———. 1988b. "Movimiento de Mujeres en América Latina: Un Reto para el Análisis y para la Acción." In *Mujeres, Crisis y Movimiento: América Latina y el Caribe.* Ediciones de las Mujeres, No. 9. Santiago: Isis Internacional. 83–90.
———. 1990. "Women, Vote for Yourselves." In *Third World/Second Sex*, ed. Miranda Davies. Vol. 2. London: Zed. 42–9.
———. 1991. "El Movimiento Feminista Latinoamericano: Entre la Esperanza y el Desencanto" (Apuntes para el debate). *El Cielo por Asalto* 2 (Fall): 9–24.
Vásquez, Ana. "Dudas y Contradicciones." 1985. *Nueva Sociedad* 78 (July/August): 55–61.
Vega, H. 1984. *Crisis Económica, Estabilidad y Deuda Externa. Un Pronóstico Económico para el Análisis Político.* Documento de Trabajo, No. 33. Santiago: PET.
Vergara, Pilar. 1982. "La Transformaciónes del Estado Chileno bajo el Régimen Militar." *Revista Mexicana de Socología.* México: Universidad Nacional Autónoma de México, April/June. 65–104.
———. 1986. "Changes in the Economic Functions of the Chilean State under the Military Regime." In *Military Rule in Chile. Dictatorship and Opposition*, ed. J. Samuel Valenzuela and Arturo Valenzuela. Baltimore: Johns Hopkins Press. 85–116.
Volk, Steven. 1983. "The Lessons and Legacy of a Dark Decade." *NACLA Report* (Sept./Oct.): 2–14.
———. 1988. "Chile: The Right to Coup." *NACLA Report* 5 (Sept./Oct.): 4–6.
Von Mettenheim, Kurt and James Malloy, ed. 1988. *Deepening Democracy in Latin America.* Pittsburgh: University of Pittsburgh Press.
Walton, Gary M., ed. 1985. *The National Economic Policies of Chile.* Connecticut: Jai Press.
West, Guida and Rhoda Lois Blumberg. 1990. "Reconstructing Social Protest from a Feminist Perspective." In *Women and Social Protest*, ed. Guida West and Rhoda Lois Blumberg. New York: Oxford University Press. 3–35.
West, Guida and Rhoda Lois Blumberg, eds. 1990. *Women and Social Protest.* New York: Oxford University Press.

Index

Allende Government
  and women, 22
  backlash against, 23
  support for, 23
Aylwin Government
  and grassroots organizations, 108
  policy toward women, 91, 93, 94, 113

Casas de la Mujer, 119
Catholic church
  aid for the victims of repression, 48
  and ollas, 107
  church organizations, 49, 51
Centro de Servicios y Promoción de la Mujer (DOMOS), 118
Centro El Canelo de Nos, 119
Centros de Madres
  Allende government and, 22
  military government and, 25
  PDC and, 18
  the miliatary government, 31
Chile
  Catholic church in, 49, 51
  culture, 18
  democracy in, 74
  democratic transition, 82
  economic crisis in, 79
  elections in, 89
  health system in, 42
  patriarchal model, 28
  political parties in, 113
  subordination of women, 27
  transition to democracy, 76, 86
  women's movement in, 59, 76, 99
Class
  and gender, 117
  inequities in the distribution of wealth, 41
  marginalization of the poor, 38
  political polarization, 23
  popular sectors, 38, 45, 47, 50, 62, 72, 91, 107
Comisión Chilena de Derechos Humanos, 65
Comisión de Derechos de la Mujer, 75
Community organizations, 18
Concertación, 93, 94
  agenda for women, 93
  policies of, 95
Concertación de Partidos por la Democracia, 90, 91
Concertación Nacional de las Mujeres por la Democracia, 90

Discrimination against women, 74
  in Chilean law, 45
Division of labor, 26

Economic crisis
  of 1981, 38
Education
  sexual discrimination in, 44

Family
  and neo liberal model, 40
  and ollas, 70
  and the church, 52
  and women, 27, 28, 39, 53, 60, 66, 87
  authoritarianism in, 29, 53
  gender-specific roles in, 40
  implications of socialism for, 23
  patriarchal, 111
  social services, 42
  women's domain, 26

Health
  birth control, 42
  privatization of health services, 42
Housing

under the military regime, 43
Under the military regime, 43
Human rights
  abuses, 65
  and the Catholic Church, 49, 64
  and the military, 59, 106
  and women, 46, 64, 75, 95, 105
  groups and the church, 50
  investigations of violations, 106
  reparations, 95, 105, 106

Institutionalization
  of Pinochet's authoritarian plan, 25
  of the regime, 38
  women's movement, 59, 122

Jornada por el Derecho a la Democracia, 76

Left
  split in, 87
  split in, 80
Legal status
  of women, 44

Military government, 37
  and the church, 48
  and the popular sectors, 34
  crisis of legitimacy, 80
  cultural project, 72
  destatization, 25
  education, 44
  health system, 42
  housing, 43
  indoctrination, 31, 32, 35
  inequities in the distribution of wealth, 41
  institutional transition, 80, 81, 88
  maternal role of women, 27
  official organizations, 24, 30, 33
  opposition to, 54, 61
  patriarchal model, 28, 40, 46
  personalization of leadership, 38
  policies of, 37, 41, 45, 49, 59, 79
  repression, 38, 80, 82
  socio-economic policies of, 37
  termination of social services, 42
  women's organizations, 22
  women's support for, 31
Moral feminism, 18
Mujeres por la Democracia, 89
Mujeres Unidas por el NO, 89

National Commission on Truth and Reconciliation, 105
National security doctrine
  adherence to role designation, 28
Neo-liberal model, 38

Ollas
  role in post-military period, 108

Plebiscite in 1988, 81
Political participation
  of Chilean women, 17
  of women, 30, 93, 113
Political parties
  and social movements, 83
  and the military government, 81
  as mediators between state and society, 79, 86
  demands, 82
  department for women, 111, 112
  opposition to the regime, 80, 89
  positive discrimination, 92, 111, 112, 113
  return of, 79, 80, 87
  role in transition, 83
  social movements, 79, 86
  the women's movement, 64, 84, 85, 86, 93, 94, 110
  women's representation in, 114
Popular organizations, 74
Popular Unity government, 22
Private and the public, 53, 87
Proyecto ROCAP, 108
Public and the private, 60

Repression
  and the military, 38

Research
  on women's issues, 118
Right (ideology) and women, 113
Rights of women, 119, 121

Separation of the public and the
  private, 27
SERNAM
  proposals, 102
Social movements
  and political parties, 83
  and the state, 99
  informal networks, 46

Tierra Nuestra, 119

unemployment
  neo-liberal economic experiment,
    39
Unidad de Comunicación
  Alternativa de la Mujer, 120
Unión de Mujeres de Chile, 117
Unión de Mujeres Socialistas, 111

Violence against women, 74
Voluntariado Nacional, 33

Women's movement
  alternative vision of society, 122
  and Concertación, 94, 95
  and political parties, 64, 80, 82, 84,
    85, 86, 87, 91, 96, 110, 112, 114
  and the AD, 88
  as a social movement, 100
  Campaigns, 121
  consciousness-raising, 115, 117,
    118
  critique, 52, 53, 54, 59
  critique of patriarchy, 87
  cultural change, 85, 86, 114
  decentralization, 99, 115

  demands, 74, 80, 85, 88, 89
  democratic state, 100, 103
  diversity, 59, 74, 90, 96, 100, 115,
    121
  human rights strand, 59
  institutionalization of, 59, 114
  new form of doing politics, 66, 72
  opposition to the regime, 54, 64,
    73, 74, 76, 88, 89
  political parties, 87
  public and private, 71
  rise of, 37, 45, 48, 54
  strands within, 76, 115, 116
  strategies, 85, 96, 100
  subordination of women's goals to
    the struggle for democracy, 89
  suffrage rights, 17
  tensions between feministas and
    políticas, 63, 64, 84, 99
  transition to democracy, 88, 99,
    121
Women's organizations
  and informal networks, 47
  campaigns, 121
  education, 119, 120
  feminist groups, 59, 60, 62, 63, 74,
    114, 115, 117, 118, 121, 122
  gender-specific services, 118, 120
  grassroots organizations, 67, 119
  human rights groups, 59, 64, 65,
    95, 96, 115
  international assistance, 118
  neighborhood-based organizations,
    59
  popular organizations, 109
  prior to 1973, 22
  protests, 75, 76
  publications, 120
  research, 120, 121
  roots of, 47, 48
  sobrevivencia organizations, 107